Advance Praise
for *Holy Everything*

Whether Emily uses tomatoes or bee colonies - she teaches us about faith by pointing out the simple, lovely experiences of life. She has an approachable and guiding voice to her writing and this collection of essays is testament to that. A pastor, writer and bold woman, Emily's words will be an inspiration to all who read them.
- ELIZABETH MCBRIDE, editor of *Café Magazine* and director of Intergenerational Programs for Women of the ELCA

Every day of our life is precious. How we live matters. Pastor Emily reminds us with her stories to seek joy, experience wonder and feel gratitude. She invites us to fill up our lifetime with kindness, love and faith.
- LOREN ELSE, Columnist for the *Rochester Post-Bulletin*

Pastor Emily takes the normal mundane daily tasks and occurrences by giving them a twist of fun and nostalgia. But more importantly she causes the reader to pause and reflect on their place in this world to appreciate life's precious moments.
- KEVIN TORGERSON, Sheriff of Olmsted County

For the past several years, Pastor Emily Carson has been writing a weekly column in the Rochester Post-Bulletin in which she shares how she sees the presence of God in a variety of life's experiences.
I am thrilled that Emily has now brought these columns together in her new book, *Holy Everything*. Under headings such as joy, gratitude, Jesus, nature, pause, church, peace, justice, and change, Emily's stories invite us to see the holy in our own life experiences.
I recommend using *Holy Everything* as a daily meditational resource, reading one story each day, letting that day's story invite you into reflection on where you see the holy in your own life experiences. That's what I plan to do.
- STEVEN H DELZER, Bishop of Southeastern Minnesota Synod of the ELCA

Emily reminds us-even in the smallest ways- there is a bit of holy in much of our everyday lives if we remember to look for it.
-TRACY MCCRAY, host of Mayo Clinic Radio

Holy Everything

Emily Carson

www.9footvoice.com

9 Foot Voice - Minnesota

Dedicated to all those who encourage curiosity.

Contents

Introduction - xi
The Greatest Antidote

Joy - 1
Tomato Tears
Happiness Pie
The Mysterious Metal Box
Sitting Joyfully in the Bathroom Closet
The Earl of Soil
Note to Self
Hear Comes the Sun
The Sweetest Score

Gratitude - 21
Giant Package of Sunshine
Thankful for Everything
Leading Us Home
Year One
Amen, Ed
Gratitude Tears — *Leaving Zion*

Jesus - 37
Unboxing _the gift first_
More than Muscles — _Strength_
Good News? _Justice_
Mystery upon Mystery _- Communion_
Graduates: This One's for You
Changing Winds

Nature - 55
Training a Female Pheasant
Holy Truths
Being Superior
Lady Returns
The Aisle of Seeds
Seasonally Yours
Seasonal Magic
A Delicious Discovery
The Whispering Desert
Tiny Eternity

Pause - 77
Breathing Break
Window Washing
Electronic Overwhelm
The First Frost
Be Calm
The Perfect Shoes
Ordinary Time

Church - 97

Curators of Curiosity
Living Waters
Book of Faith
In Some Sacred Past
A Prairie of Negativity
A New Chapter
Stewards of the Mysteries of God
I Will Pray for You
Faith and Doubt
Peace Exchange

Peace - 123

SMASH!
The Courage to Disagree
Releasing Worry
Surrounded by Noise
Default Settings
A Global Reset
The Peace and Unity of Christ
We Lost our Words

Justice - 145

The Entitlement Hulk
News Fatigue
Great America
Pipestone
A Song of Joy in Your Heart
Build this World from Love
Use Your Power
Shamar the Earth

Change - 169
Curveballs
It's Not All Rainbows, Sparklers and Rainbows
Hibernating on the Fence
Anniversaries of Loss
Funeral Orchids
The Compass
Goodbye, House

You - 187
Love Yourself
Be Yourself
Your Real, Whole Self
You Are You
Look Up and Jump Out
The Unconventional Bear

Us - 203
We Need Help
Accidentally Imprinted
God Is Love
Finn, the Dog
The Greatest Joy
Don't Spoil the Beauty of this Place
She Was My Girl
Every Story of Your Whole Life
Pride, the Swan

Acknowledgements - 227

Introduction

The Greatest Antitode

Writing is the greatest antidote I've found to fear. When I have a pen in my hand or a keyboard under my fingers, I feel brave and open. Stringing words together is medicine to my soul, and it always has been.

I grew up in Iowa and began journaling the summer before third grade. When I wasn't reflecting about boys, I was referencing "Brand New Lives" (BNLs). I don't remember my initial inspiration for regularly starting BNLs so early on in my own story, but they've been a regular part of my existence since elementary school. An eager learner ever-ready to explore a new idea, I'd start a Brand New Life whenever I encountered a particularly impactful nugget of wisdom that I wanted to implement.

A new season of life always required a fresh clean page of paper in my journal with "BNL" written in capital letters at the top of the page. I guess I've always been compelled by the idea that people can reclaim their stories and begin again anytime.

Since 2011, the Rochester Post-Bulletin has given me a weekly spot in the newspaper to explore ideas about the intersections of spirituality and daily life. Those reflections now comprise this book, *Holy Everything*. I hope it will be a thought-provoking companion for your journey.

The book is structured around different themes. As you dig into the pages ahead, please utilize this text in whatever way is most helpful to you. Read it from beginning to end, use it as a daily devotional, or select essays within the themes most intriguing to you as you navigate your own BNLs.

Thank you for your readership and for trusting me with your invaluable neurons and synapses. I pray the ideas you encounter in this book will empower you to feel courageous, curious and compassionate.

Holy Everything

Joy

Tomato Tears

I had two sacred encounters with tomatoes last week. The first happened during my lunch break.

I grabbed a tomato from the church garden on my way home, thinking I'd throw some slices on a sandwich. My brain was in a million places that day, consumed with thoughts of my to-do list, broken car, and unmet summer goals. On my drive home for lunch, I had to remind myself of two of my most recent life goals: slow down and eat real food.

But when I got home, I cut off a small slice of the tomato to test it out, and, for a few moments, everything stopped. It was like a dose of heaven had been injected right into my mouth. Time froze as I chewed, and my worries evaporated. My heart exploded with gratitude for the food in front of me. I decided to forgo my sandwich plan and eat the tomato whole instead. The rest of the day dripped with the wonder of that precious garden produce.

Over the weekend, I experienced my second sacred tomato moment. I had a big bowl of tomatoes on the counter but no idea what to do with them. I decided I'd chop them all up and then make a plan.

This haphazard approach in the kitchen is reflective of my general inability to follow recipes or accurately menu plan (needless to say, I eat a lot of oatmeal).

As I cut the red, juicy tomatoes into pieces, I was suddenly overcome with memories of my grandma who died in 2002. Verona loved tomatoes. A plate of tomatoes often sat on her kitchen table in the late summer. A jar of sugar was always nearby to sprinkle on top. Her tomato soup was perfection.

Returning to the reality of my own kitchen, I felt a few tears streaming down my cheeks. They were the kind of happy/sad tears that I think of as a special sort of holy water.

We all spill them from time to time, tears that are a combination of thankfulness and sadness. My tomato tears were certainly both. I was happy for the memories of my grandma, but sad for the reality that she isn't on earth anymore.

I ended up using the tomatoes to make my first-ever batch of tomato soup. I don't know what my grandma's recipe was, but, somehow, mine tasted like hers and I loved every spoonful.

It's funny. I teach and preach about God's nearness every day, but, in my own life, I often forget. I suppose we all fail to notice life's tomato moments from time to time.

But maybe you don't like tomatoes or soup or gardening. No problem. None of those elements are required. God is all around, all the time.

This week, savor the details of your life. Take note of those precious moments when something ordinary transforms into a holy reminder that every day is a treasure.

Happiness Pie

It started mid-evening on Friday. There was a new and sudden desire in my heart.

"I'm going to make a pie!" I proclaimed to the kitchen.

I was expecting some company at my house the next day. Historically, I have never provided homemade baked goods for guests. But my mom often does. And my Grandma Verona always did, too. I felt inspired to become a hospitable hostess and carry on the family tradition. The moment had finally arrived, just 30 years in the making.

It was pie time.

Thankfully, I didn't have to look far for a recipe. I collect cookbooks. Why? I'm not sure. I like them in theory more than in practice. Older, used cookbooks strike my fancy most of all. They carry so much history and experience. I reached way up in the cupboard and located *The Better Homes and Gardens Cookbook*, 1953 edition.

Now it was time to decide. What kind of pie?

Feeling brave, I decided on lemon meringue. Next stop: the grocery store. I needed to buy lemons, butter, and eggs. Amazingly, the other ingredients were already waiting for me in the pantry.

As I wandered through the grocery store, my heart was pitter-pattering with excitement. "I'm making a pie tonight!" I wanted to say to every single person I encountered (but somehow held my tongue).

At the checkout counter, Danika was working. She's a terrific high school student and church member. "What are you up to tonight?" she asked. Dear Danika! So kind! I was hoping she'd ask.

"I'm making my first pie."

"I did that once," she said with a grin.

"Awesome! That's amazing! What kind?" Since she was clearly a pie pro, I hoped she'd share some wisdom.

"Strawberry rhubarb. It wasn't pretty, but it tasted good."

It was a nice dose of encouragement. Even if my pie did not win for most photographic, perhaps it would still be edible.

Back at home, the process of getting all the ingredients on the counter made me feel a twinge anxious. I thought about putting it off to watch old episodes of *Dawson's Creek* instead. But no. It was pie time and there was no backing out.

I followed all the instructions for the recipe. This, in itself, was a major feat. Water, sugar and cornstarch. Stir it together nonstop for awhile over heat, add some lemony goodness, and poof - pie filling! There was a lot of shrieking with joy throughout the process.

The meringue-making was exciting, too. Who knew? A hand mixer plus egg whites plus sugar equals happiness.

As the pie cooked in the oven, I decided it was time to tell the universe. After sufficiently documenting the pie via email, Facebook, text message and Instagram, I paused for a moment. In all the excitement, I'd totally forgotten something.

I was not the first person to ever make a pie.

My grandma, Verona, made pies. My mother, Pam, made pies. Danika made a pie! And for generations before them, dedicated, loving women and men have been making pies. Their baking experiences probably didn't get described in detail. Photos likely went unsnapped. They may or may not have received affirmation for their hard work. But they made the pies anyway because they loved to feed something delicious to their friends and families.

I hope I told Grandma how much I loved it when she made her amazing pies. Strawberry rhubarb. Graham cracker. Apple. I hope I said thanks.

I know I've only made one pie so far, but I have a strong feeling that this is just the start of a joyful new Friday night tradition.

The Mysterious
Metal Box

There are enjoyable moments of each day. But there is one particular ritual I always look forward to: getting the mail.

I was first invited to go and get the mail around the age of seven. We lived in the country at the time, and it was a small jaunt from the house to the end of the driveway.

I never knew what I would find when I opened the mysterious metal box, and the adventure was exhilarating. Would there be colorful advertisements? Bills? Small packages? A few times a year I'd even find something addressed to me! Thrill of thrills!

My childlike fascination with the mailbox has been a consistent feature of my life at every stage. In college, two students shared one mailbox. My partner and I didn't know each other. As a way to get to know her, I sent her a card freshman year. We discovered we both liked receiving mail so much that we became modified pen-pals throughout our college experience.

In seminary, I had a mailbox on the top row. This required the use of a step-stool each day. That always made the mail-retrieving process extra fun! Plus, the seminary mailroom was a great communal space where I was always sure to run into someone interesting.

Nowadays, I have a mailbox at the end of my driveway, and opening it is the way I end each workday. Stopping to get the mail is the last thing I do before pulling into the garage each night.

With all the joy I have surrounding the U.S. Postal Service, you'd think I must have a lot of pen-pals or other sources of exciting mail. I don't. Mostly, I receive the same things you receive: bills, bonus coupons, and advertisements.

But now and then there really is a treasure in there! A letter. A package. A free sample. I'm usually so excited, I tear it open outside! I can't even wait until I get into the house! The anticipation gets me every time.

I have no idea why I enjoy getting the mail so much, but I hope I never lose that feeling. Joy is such a powerful emotion. It is a gift from God. Many of the biblical Psalms are full of references to joy, inviting people to sing for joy, clap for joy, and leap for joy.

Experiencing exuberant joy is part of being human. We all benefit from feeling true delight in some form every single day. Sometimes happy experiences come right to us, handed on a platter. But oftentimes we have to seek them out, searching the mundane to find something jubilant.

I hope you find a reason to leap for joy this week. And who knows? Perhaps the motivation will be only a mailbox away.

Sitting Joyfully in the Bathroom Closet

"There's no use crying over spilled milk," the adage goes.

But what about broken china? Is that tear-worthy?

During a recent morning of downsizing my possession piles, I visited our basement closet-of-all-things seeking more clothing items to give away. Upon entry into the long and narrow space, I was dismayed to find a box of china that had tipped over. Apparently my stacking method was just as precarious as it appeared.

Several pieces had broken in the fall. Based on this experience, I'd shift the ol' spilled milk guidance to something like, "Feel free to cry over broken china and then use the rest of the non-broken pieces as often as you can."

Clearly, the extended version has less of a ring to it, but the sentiment remains. It's time to use the belongings we have and release the rest.

So that is what we're doing. I've been moving much of our boxed specialty ware into the regular household rotation. Snacks? They will now be served on vintage glassware. Having a cup of tea? Might as well put a saucer with that cup because why else are we keeping this stack of saucers around? Friends coming over for a casual dinner? They better get ready, because grilled pizza is even more fun on silver-rimmed dinner plates!

From an early age, I've had a strong desire to save special things instead of just using and enjoying them. It started with particularly favorite clothes and then moved on to pens, notebooks, toys, mugs, towels, dishware and even ingredients in the cupboard. Aspects of this inclination make sense - it stems from the hope of having special things around for special moments.

In my case, though, it's also rooted in a misguided sense of scarcity. Let's take writing utensils as an example. Are my favorite pens somehow better off sitting untouched on my desk while I instead use up the ink in the pens I don't like? No way! I'm done with that illogical approach to life. The time has come to enjoy the possessions I have and give away the rest.

My friend, April, replied to a post that I shared online about this topic. She reflected, "We just pulled out our wedding silverware for the very first time a month ago! Almost 14 years unused, and now I get to remember the joy of registering for it every day!"

Isn't that a beautiful idea? Whether you've been saving your wedding china or your favorite blouse or your grandma's brooch or your dad's favorite hammer, maybe now's the time to start enjoying your treasures!

Or maybe it's not a physical object that you've been hiding away for the right time. Instead, perhaps you've been saving up your real feelings or your gratitude or your true vocational desires or an adventure you've been dreaming about for decades. In those cases, the question still remains: if not now, when?

One of the pieces of china from the closet broke perfectly in half. No shards. Just a clean break. I saved it and asked my husband, Justin, if he had any ideas. Craft project? Garden ornament? In the end, I found the perfect spot for the half-plate. It's now holding cotton pads and sitting joyfully in the bathroom closet - a space I look at everyday as I get ready in the morning. Its placement serves as a daily reminder to stop waiting for perfect occasions and instead rejoice in the moment at hand - a moment that by its mere existence is more than special enough to merit the use of anything in our household.

The Earl of Soil

Cucumbers and tomatoes for breakfast. That's my game plan for the rest of the summer - or at least as long as our garden bounty continues.

It seems like magic. In May, we put seeds and tiny plants into the ground, then get to watch them transform into edible wonders a few months later. It feels lavish and almost unreal. How fabulous!

When my taste buds encounter something I helped to grow, the experience makes me feel like a queen. It's like getting a front-row seat in the Royal Court of Creation, joining the Earl of Soil, Duchess of Sunshine and Jester of Rain as we all rejoice in the banquet in our midst.

This wonderment is why I go outside and gaze upon our fairly small garden every morning. No matter what else happens that day, I know I've already experienced something extraordinary. The morning continues with sliced cucumber and coffee.

My husband, Justin, is in charge of coffee. He's an expert at preparing it, and I'm mediocre, so in the household division of labor, caffeine-prep rests firmly with him. I wouldn't say he's as into eating garden produce for breakfast (he's more of a traditionalist, preferring eggs or oatmeal), but he savors our veggies for lunch, dinner, and snacks.

A few weeks back, on the night before I pulled the first cucumber and tomato, I had butterflies of the pre-harvest variety. Excitement. Anticipation. Awe. I had been watching the ripening fruits for weeks as they'd grown. I knew that as soon as I woke up, it would be time: Christmas in July!

I woke up at the crack of dawn and walked out to the garden in my turquoise pajamas. Morning dew tickled my toes. It's a delight to walk around in the yard barefoot in the summer (though I do recommend putting on shoes if you're moving deck furniture; but that's a story for another day, maybe after the swelling in my ankle has receded).

I kneeled at the garden. First, I gently tugged on the ruby red tomato; then I yanked a medium-sized green cucumber from its vine.

When I walked back into the house, I grabbed a cutting board and my favorite knife then got to slicing. Justin and I both immediately dug into the sweet wedges of tomato and fresh-as-rain cucumber.

"There is nothing like a tomato from the garden," he said. I enthusiastically agreed. It was a marvelous start to a Thursday.

"How's your summer going?" It's a question folks often ask one another this time of year before trading familiar refrains. "It's moving so fast! I can't believe it's July!" or "Where's the summer gone?" All those sentiments feel so true. It's hard not to want to grasp this precious season and force it to stay permanently. But that's just not the way seasons work.

This is a gift of the garden: it slows me down. It wakes me up to the present moment. It invites me to pay attention to tiny flowering blossoms and busy bees. It is not an exaggeration to say that watching the garden grow is one of the highlights of my entire summer. To be honest, I wouldn't have it any other way. It's nice to feel like a queen.

Note to Self

I've long been drawn to the concept of a daily journal, but in practice, I've missed far more days (and years) than I've recorded. Add in a penchant for cute notebooks (and the desire to get a new one every time I start journaling again), and, before you know it, I have two giant boxes of barely used notebooks chronicling the last 20 years.

Elaine, a friend of mine, has been keeping a daily diary for many decades. Inspiring! It is not only a great source for future reference, it is also a way to honor the gifts of each day. Juliet, another amazing woman and friend, wrote her autobiography at the age of 80; she's now 102. Reading it a few weeks back was a source of great joy. In it, she writes that if she could go back and do it all again, she'd likely keep a journal because it would make things easier to remember.

Inspired by the ample wisdom and experience of Elaine and Juliet, I am now renewed in my resolve to keep a regular written record of encounters, emotions, and activities.

But before choosing a new writing pad, I thought it might be fun to dig through my childhood diaries. I wrote regularly from the ages of 10-18. Up until a week ago, I hadn't read them for a long while. As I opened the first page, I wondered if perhaps I'd discover something new or surprising about my young self. What I discovered is that the 10-year-old Emily is surprisingly similar to the 30-year-old version.

A sampling:

March 1, 1996 (age 12): *Today I went to my Grandma's with my mom and my brother. It was fun, just like it always is.*
Spending time with my mom and brother is still among my very favorite activities, and I miss Grandma a lot - especially during rhubarb season.

May 15, 1996 (age 12): *I am listening to "Nobody Knows" by The Tony Rich Project. It is a very sad song, and I have no idea why I listen to it so often.*
I still listen to beautiful, sad songs on repeat.

May 16, 1996 (age 12): *I wonder if I will be a good kisser or a bad kisser. And do you just learn how as you go along?*
Perhaps this is one of the more significant developments of the last 18 years. I did finally figure out one of life's biggest mysteries: the first kiss. But it took a few more years of pining away. To bide my time, I watched the 1996 film version of "Romeo and Juliet," starring Leonardo DiCaprio and Claire Danes, repeatedly.

August 21, 1996 (age 13): *As long as I get to sleep at 10:30 p.m., I will get at least eight hours of sleep.*
What can I say? Adequate sleep has always been very important to me.

Reading through my old entries nudged me forward in picking up the practice once again. It was especially interesting to read about my perceptions of God, faith, and church throughout those teen years. It was a time of real development. Maybe at 40 or 50, I'll look back at this chapter of life in the same way, as a time of great learning.

A journal can take many forms. Entries don't need to be long. You can call it whatever you want: a daily record, a journal, a diary. You can write in a book or use an app on your phone. At its core, a journal is a way to highlight moments, special and ordinary. It's a way to say, "God, I'm grateful for this life. Here are some bits I want to remember." It doesn't need to be shared or edited. There are no rules.

Of course, a journal is just one of many ways to pause and take note of this outstanding life we've been given. What are some ways you might pause in the months ahead? Whatever you choose, it will be time well spent.

Here Comes the Sun

The pre-excitement started a while ago. Advance tickets were purchased, and then I prepared my beloved clipboard with all the most important documents (site map, parking map, "favorites" list and a schedule of events). Fast forward a few weeks and add in a couple hours on Interstate 35... and presto: The Iowa State Fair!

My sweetheart, Justin, and I found a yard to park in near the fairgrounds and hiked over to the entrance gate. He's a fellow Iowa native, which made him a perfect co-adventurer for the day. He's also one of the very few people on the planet who doesn't seem to mind having a girlfriend who carries a clipboard for personal enjoyment.

Justin was an FFA member in high school and spent several summers working shows at the grandstand and living in the on-site dormitory. Though the layout of the grounds has expanded a bit since then, he definitely remembered his way around.

We went from building to building. As we walked through one of the barns, we got a special behind-the-scenes glimpse of the teenage girls getting ready to ride their horses for the Cowgirl Queen Contest. The woodworking and photography displays were highlights, but each stop along the way offered its own flair (and people-watching).

The best moment of all came at the end of the day. We found our way over to Pioneer Hall. The Midway volume had increased vastly by that point, as had the number of fairgoers. I was getting a little overwhelmed. At Pioneer Hall, there were antiques to peruse, while a band called R.B.J. was playing hits from the 1950s and '60s. After admiring the items inside, we stepped back into the summer evening. There was a big, old house just steps away called the Ralph H. Deets Historical Museum. Neither of us had ever noticed it before. It was closing time there, and the lights were switching off as we walked closer.

"Oh, darn," I said. "We just missed it. But maybe we could just sit down anyway."

Lovely wooden rockers lined the wrap-around porch. We plopped down to rest a while. Glancing across the way through the open barn door, we realized we had a perfect view of the stage inside Pioneer Hall. It felt like R.B.J. was playing us a private concert as they harmonized to "Here Comes the Sun." The rest of the fair noise faded to the background.

Rocking back and forth on the porch, the lyrics of the song felt truer than ever:

> *Little darling, the smile's returning to the faces,*
> *little darling, it seems like years since it's been here.*
> *Here comes the sun, here comes the sun,*
> *and I say, it's alright.*

"This has been a great summer," I reflected. "And this is a really great fair."

The Sweetest Score

My record collection got a boost a few weeks ago when my Uncle Darrel was in town. He gifted me a 1951 edition of "Rudolph the Red-Nosed Reindeer" that he picked up at a thrift shop. The album is a single, so each listen requires picking up the tone-arm and shifting it back to the outer ring.

While I could certainly utilize my record player any time of year, it spins most frequently during December. I love when the sounds of Bing Crosby and Nat King Cole fill the house in the evenings.

But the music of Christmas is a special ornament on the holiday tree, regardless of how we play it. Last Sunday afternoon I helped lead worship at St. Mark's Lutheran Home in Austin. Together, we joyfully sang some of their favorites: "O Come All Ye Faithful," "Go Tell It on the Mountain," and "Joy to the World." It was moving to witness the depth to which these hymns were rooted in the residents. Even though memory had become hazy for some, they could still give voice to these familiar hymns.

Another musical highlight was last weekend's Christmas at Assisi concert at Assisi Heights. Both the Choral Arts Ensemble and the high school Honors Choir sang pieces from an array of genres. The immense beauty of Lourdes Chapel was a perfect backdrop. Each line of music was delivered with care and passion by the musicians.

The evening concluded with artistic director Rick Kvam's arrangement of Franz Gruber's "Stille Nacht."

"This is one of my favorites," Justin whispered in my ear as the lights came down. By the time the choirs began singing, the chapel was completely darkened save the flickering lights of the candles up front. I nuzzled my head onto Justin's shoulder and closed my eyes. The voices of all the choir members were like angels carrying me to a sacred space; a space where all of life is an interconnected web of gratitude.

My evening at Assisi wrapped up in the best way I can imagine: Justin and I got engaged! He proposed after the concert in the courtyard outside my office at Assisi Heights. Now whenever I look out my office window, I am reminded of the kind and loving words he spoke as we embarked on this new chapter in our relationship.

The score of life has a variety of movements. This one is utterly sweet, and I'm savoring every note.

Gratitude

Giant Package
of Sunshine

Sometimes life presents us with unexpected opportunities to express gratitude to people for the impact they've made on our lives. When these occasions come up, it's well worth seizing the chance to say a concrete, "Thank you."

Last week, I had just such an encounter with one of my favorite teachers, Mrs. Thomas, and her husband, Larry. (Her first name is Colleen, but as with any teacher, she will always be Mrs. Thomas to me.) They live in my hometown of Dunkerton, Iowa, and happened to be driving through the Rochester area on the way back from vacation.

Thanks to the wonders of Facebook, Mrs. Thomas was able to send a quick message asking if I'd be available to meet up on their way through town. I invited them to come to Assisi Heights where our Southeastern Minnesota Synod offices are located. It is a beautiful, castle-like structure on a hill.

My heart raced with excitement. I hadn't seen these two special people in person since high school graduation almost 15 years ago! I felt a sudden urge to tidy up my desk area, organize my oversized collection of writing utensils, and appear as responsible as possible. I announced to my co-worker, Gwen, "I can hardly believe it! One of my very favorite teachers is going to be stopping by shortly. I'm a little nervous!"

Within an hour, Colleen and Larry had arrived. Hugs were exchanged. Photos were snapped. For some sacred sunshine moments, we all sat together in the flower-filled courtyard of Assisi Heights catching up. There was something wholly (and holy) disarming about coming face-to-face with a person I'd known in another season of life but hadn't seen for a long time. It was like the past made a surprise appearance in the present and different life chapters got a chance to meet and overlap.

Mrs. Thomas was my first homeroom teacher in seventh grade. She taught Health and Family Consumer Science for middle and high school, and she was also the mother of one of my good pals, Trent. Qualities I have always admired about her: she is a huge wellness and exercise advocate, she is perpetually encouraging and upbeat, and (to my memory) she never lost her temper in the classroom. Her disposition made a significant imprint on me. Mrs. Thomas' educational leadership helped me identify that I wanted to be the kind of person who always made it a priority to encourage other people.

We exchanged stories for awhile, and I became teary-eyed thinking about how unexpected and special it was to be sitting with them. Sometimes it's like God delivers a giant package of sunshine on the doorstep without any notice at all. Not all the time, of course. Other times it's more like a giant package of excrement. Life can be a real smorgasbord of deliveries. But I'd prefer a package of sunshine over a package of poo any day, and on that particular afternoon last week, I got sunshine. Thanks be to God.

As our time together was coming to a close, it was time to share the words that had been waiting on just the other side of my lips.

"Thank you for being a really special influence in my life," I said.

"You are so very welcome, Emily," Mrs. Thomas said with the same kind eyes and gracious smile I'd seen nearly every day growing up.

People shape people. We impact each other's lives in large ways and small all the time. Every now and then we get a chance to say, "Thanks for being you," to some of those shapers. Seize a chance to say a concrete word of gratitude at some point this week. And may we always find time to say thanks to God for the gift of impactful connections throughout our lives.

Thankful for Everything

With Thanksgiving just around the corner, it's a marvelous week to practice gratitude. More than just being a pleasant habit, cultivating an attitude of thankfulness has actual health benefits. Research has shown that gratitude is a strong determinant of overall well-being. Gratefulness is also associated with increased ability to cope, better sleep, economic generosity and decreased stress.

Author Anne Lamott writes about thankfulness in her book, <u>Help Thanks Wow: Three Essential Prayers</u>. About the interesting connection between gratitude and service to others, she reflects,

Gratitude begins in our hearts and then dovetails into behavior. It almost always makes you willing to be of service, which is where the joy resides… When you are aware of all that has been given to you, in your lifetime and the past few days, it is hard not to be humbled, and pleased to give back.

For some people, gratitude is deeply rooted in their sense of spirituality. The individual who composed Psalm 100 writes, "Enter God's gates with thanksgiving and God's courts with praise, give thanks to the Lord and praise God's name." The Psalm is an invitation to be thankful to God for everything.

Gratefulness rooted in a sense of God is one approach to thanksgiving. However, one need not be religious or spiritual in order to be grateful. I find this to be one of the most intriguing parts about grounding oneself in thankfulness; there are basically no other requirements than the willingness to pay attention and acknowledge that which one appreciates.

Here are a few thankfulness practices to incorporate into your life this week or anytime:

1. Each night before bed, write for two minutes (set a timer) about a specific experience during the day that brought you joy.

2. Write a letter to someone for whom you are grateful and give it to the person.

3. Incorporate a gratitude practice into an existing household routine. If you share your home with others, consider making meals a time for everyone to express something for which they're grateful.

There are a thousand other ways to incorporate thankfulness into your life. And if you're looking to start, it doesn't need to be complicated. Even simply pausing for a single minute to breathe and reflect on something for which you're grateful can reframe your whole day.

Please know how very thankful I am for each of you. It is a great gift to me be able to explore life and faith with you every week. I praise God for this opportunity and for your willingness to journey together.

A Prayer for Thanksgiving:
God who is always near,
we're grateful…
for this day,
for this meal,
for this life.
Sometimes the world feels chaotic and uncertain.
There are a host of things we don't understand.
We want to serve, but we're not always sure how.
We want to be generous, but sometimes it's hard to let go.
In the midst of all challenges,

bring us back to gratitude.
Reroot us always in this soil.
Remind us daily to slow down,
and pay attention.
Equip us to awaken to the wonder
of everything.
Give us the courage to listen to your voice,
and respond.
Amen.

Leading Us Home

There is much to love about a Christmas program. Wonderful, well-rehearsed music. Joyful children ready to proclaim their memorized lines. Devoted volunteers coordinating behind the scenes. A sanctuary full of supportive parents and grandparents.

We are in the midst of that magnificent time of year when calendars are bursting with Sunday School programs, live nativities, and holiday musical concerts. We had our Christmas program at church last Sunday. It was a 100 percent delight!

Now is a prime time to pause and reflect on the deeper value of all these seasonal events. The children who sing, play instruments, and act at holiday programs are more than precious, mini-adults. They are messengers who bring the good news of Jesus' birth to us in a myriad of ways.

I regret that in the past, sometimes my default response when seeing youngsters at a Christmas program was to immediately affirm their cuteness. Boys with tiny ties. Girls with curls. Admittedly, they are precious!

But I've realized over time that focusing comments on their sweet appearances distracts from (and perhaps even diminishes) the larger ministry they provide. They are leaders, prophets, and spokespeople of God!

For the following reasons, I give special thanks and praise for the children among us and their mission as Christmas program participants:

— They are willing to stand in front of a large group of people and proclaim the good news. It's astounding. Many adults would be too nervous to do the same. But kids often have no trouble going for it. What great role models they are for the rest of us!

Thank you, kids, for reminding us to be brave. Thank you for showing us that when we're sharing the love of Jesus with others, we don't need to be afraid. We can be bold!

— Children sing! Publicly and loud! Often at full volume. They learn choreography. And they generally don't worry about whether their neighbors sing all the right notes. Instead, they just sing joyfully and unapologetically.

Thank you, kids. Thank you for showing us that making a joyful noise is not about being the best singer in the room. It's just about opening our mouths and praising God with the voice we've been given!

— They are the stars that lead us back to Jesus. In the Gospel of Matthew, a star in the sky leads the wise men to Jesus. Without the star to follow, the wise men may have gotten distracted or lost.

This time of year, there are lots of distractions for all of us. It's easy to get lost in the midst of the holiday hullabaloo. Children's programs guide us back to the infant in the manger. To Mary and Joseph. To the birthplace of eternal hope. Thank you, kids, for leading us back home.

What a joy to follow the lead of children this time of year. They share the story of Christ's birth with courage and excitement, and they inspire us to do the same.

Year One

Justin and I celebrate one year of marriage this weekend. In addition to it being 365 days of laughter, adventure and impromptu dancing in the kitchen, I've also learned a few things. Here are ten lessons gleaned from our first year of partnership.

1. Relax
Marriage has taught me that life can be experienced more than managed. In the areas where I am most inclined to worry - other people's opinions, the cleanliness of the floors, schedule planning - Justin doesn't tend to overthink, and it's rubbing off on me.

2. Be intentional
Time moves so swiftly! With the hours needed for work and other obligations, I've learned how quickly weeks can pass without sincere spaces to connect. Whenever Justin and I do take those opportunities to have meaningful time together, it's always worth it.

3. Look for reasons to be grateful
Justin is particularly good at thanking me for small acts of helpfulness, and it gives me such a boost! I hope I extend the same thoughtfulness to him because it really makes a difference.

4. Prioritize family and friend connections

In addition to being intentional about time spent with one another, we've also experienced the gift of strong relationships with family and close friends. That network of support will be a key component of maintaining a healthy partnership.

5. Share a mutual obsession

Justin and his dog came into my life about the same time, and I imagined I'd tolerate the dog for the sake of the marriage. Little did I know how much this furry companion would come to mean to me. It has been a blast to share our canine adoration. I'll never be able to thank Justin enough for bringing Finn into my life.

6. Write notes to each other through a shared journal

This suggestion came from my friend, Rev. R Rudolf. He and Jane have been married for many decades and still seem to enjoy one another's company, so I heed his words closely. He suggested that right from the start, we keep track of the things we do and places we go together. Justin and I try to update the journal a couple times a month, and we take turns writing the entries. Hopefully, it's something we can keep up indefinitely; it's already been fun to look back over the past year.

7. Reserve compassion for each other

Prior to last summer, I lived alone. Basically, I woke up in the morning and then spent the day giving out all my energy in love and listening. I'd be empty when I finally came home. At the time, it didn't seem like that big of a deal (now I realize I would've benefited from a different approach all along). Over the past year, I've realized that I need to thoughtfully reserve energy for the end of the day in order to be able to extend my partner the same care I give the rest of the world.

8. Honor that we're not the same

Justin and I aren't the same. In many areas, we are opposite. As often as is possible, I'm trying to honor and respect our differences rather than resent them.

9. Laugh a lot and listen more

So much of existence is pretty comical and laughing boosts resilience. When we're dealing with the non-funny parts of life, what helps most is a sincerely listening ear. Justin and I seem to be at our best as a team when we're either laughing or listening.

10. Keep growing

Over the past year, we've both had opportunities to stretch our wings. It has been meaningful to encourage each other to take risks, try new things, and learn.

We're marriage newbies with so much left to learn. The dance continues; we'll figure out the steps as we go. I'm grateful to the Creator of All, the timing of the Universe and the compassion of my partner for this life that we're building. It's more than I could've dreamed.

Amen, Ed

Thanks be to God for all the audio, lighting, and visual production professionals of the world! These are the folks who generally work behind the scenes to create the perfect atmosphere for conferences and concerts. They dedicate hours upon hours to set-up, tear-down and everything in between.

I worked closely with a tech crew over the past weekend, and it was an experience I will cherish for a long, long while.

The event that precipitated this production jubilee was the Synod Assembly. It's an annual event held at Mayo Civic Center in Rochester. Some 600 folks gathered for worship, fellowship, and the official business of the synod.

This year my role focused on the technical production of the event. It was brand new territory. To call me a complete and utter technical production novice would be putting it kindly. I knew from the moment I entered the venue that the days ahead were certain to be what I like to call a "great learning experience."

Over the course of the weekend, there were wonderful elements of worship and fellowship. The days were highlighted by engaging workshops, thoughtful speakers, and gifted musicians. An abundance of people worked behind the scenes to bring the event to fruition. It was great. When it was time to head home, my heart was filled with gratitude.

Of all the joyful moments, guess what inspired the precipitation of a few happy tears: saying goodbye to the tech crew! I'd only known them for 36 hours, but every minute was impactful.

The audio/visual crew was patient, encouraging, and efficient. They were organized and kind. Also, they were all good at their jobs. Really good.

I feel permanently indebted. I want to go back and rewatch every concert, newscast, play, and film I've ever seen. Then I could appropriately thank or at least acknowledge all the people who worked behind the scenes! From now on, mark my words: I will sit in the theater until the credits have rolled to the end.

To everyone who has ever tested volumes, hauled equipment, or ventured up to the ceiling in a large crane to hang lights: thank you. To all those who have ever taken tickets, edited film, or constructed a stage: thank you.

Here's what I noticed, though: these folks aren't in it for the accolades. At the end of the assembly on Saturday, Edward, a video production professional, said, "It's about helping people have an experience, a positive experience that pulls them outside of themselves."

Amen, Ed.

I know my exposure is limited, but I'm quite certain these are some of the most humble people on earth. Amazingly gifted and completely humble. What a combination.

Seeing the way Tom, Edward, Skot, Paul, Wyatt, Ron, Chris, and Arnold went about their work gave me a serious case of happy heart. What a gift it is to meet new people and watch them shine.

Gratitude Tears

Hopeful. Excited. Tearful. All of these emotions have been filling my heart space a lot lately. I'm in the midst of a life transition.

I have been the associate pastor of Zion Lutheran Church in Stewartville for 4-1/2 years. The congregation loved and accepted me from the very first day. They were patient and encouraging as I learned what it meant to be a pastor. It has been a chapter filled with goodness and grace.

I was recently offered the opportunity to serve as a pastor in a new context. Early next month, I'll be joining the staff of the Southeastern Minnesota Synod and working at Assisi Heights in Rochester. In my new role, I'll do a lot of writing and connecting with congregations throughout the region (happy side note: this column will continue). I'm thrilled and joyful.

But I'm scared and uncertain, too. Sometimes it feels like I'm living in a transitional purgatory, the space between a known past and an unknown future.

As I walk on this uncertain ground, there is one emotion that bubbles up more than any other: gratitude. Out of nowhere, it falls over me like a warm rain in the summertime.

In these transitional weeks, I look out at the congregation on Sunday mornings and nearly lose my breath. Thankfulness fills up so much of my brain that I forget what comes next in the liturgy. Two weeks ago I even forgot to collect the offering but thankfully my colleague jumped in to help.

Watching God at work through people is as good as it gets, and I've had a front row seat! Seeing the Spirit shine through folks of every age is so special it makes me want to burst into song.

I tear up a lot lately. Gratitude tears...

...when the kids eagerly share their thoughts during the children's sermon.

...during weekly Bible study when we crowd around the table in the church library to explore God's word.

...when I look out at a sea of middle schoolers who have the kind of courage and compassion that will change the world.

...when I'm at the Care Center laughing 'til it hurts with people who remember a time before television.

...as I walk past the offices of coworkers who have shown me what teamwork is all about.

It should be noted that being a pastor hasn't always been the easiest for me. There was more than one night when I laid awake agonizing over the next day, wondering if I was the wrong woman for the job. My path was sometimes blocked by fog and fear.

I didn't realize how much I was learning during those times until the haze began to lift. Maybe emotional fog is a good catalyst for the Spirit's movement.

We all face transitions and unknowns. If you're facing one right now, breathe deep. Remember that change can be beautiful, and change can be hard. Often it is both in equal measure. But God is near.

For what has been, I bow down in thankfulness and praise. And for what will be, I lift up my heart in curiosity and delight. Thanks be to God for it all.

Jesus

UnBoxing

Whenever we hear a story about someone, our minds immediately start constructing a box around them. Oftentimes we don't even realize it's happening. We unconsciously build each side based on their appearance, agreeableness, political inclinations, economic status, and a host of other criteria. Yet, shove as we may, people are far too complex to fit.

The first time I witnessed most of my middle school and high school teachers outside of a school-related event was my graduation party. As we talked and ate egg bake and Jello-cake, suddenly I realized that my beloved teachers were actual, multidimensional human beings with interests, hobbies, and lives outside the classroom. A teacher is more than a teacher. A nurse is more than a nurse. A line cook is more than a line cook. A mail carrier is more than a mail carrier. A job is only one side of an individual's infinitely sided box.

Jesus doesn't fit neatly into a box either. Try as we may to label him exclusively as Savior, Healer, or Son of God, no box can contain him. An exercise which highlights Jesus' multidimensional nature is reading the entire Gospel of Mark and then reading the entire Gospel of John. When you finish reading them both, you may well find yourself wondering, "Are these books about the same guy?" Jesus' tone and way of interacting are markedly different between the two New Testament books. This has partly to do with the fact that the books were written by different people in different centuries. But it also highlights that Jesus has a lot of layers, and no one version of the story can fully capture his essence.

There is a tendency among Christians to place Jesus wholly in the box of Comforter. We like to feel his love and acceptance and grace. We like to see artwork displaying his compassionate presence with children. We enjoy hearing stories of him feeding and healing large groups of people. All of these stories about Jesus portray really important components of his identity. It is a tremendous gift that he is truly our great advocate and healer.

But if we focus solely on Jesus as Comforter, we miss out on a lot of the other reasons why we follow him. A trip through the Gospel of Mark reveals a Jesus who:

+ despises hypocrisy;
+ spends the majority of his time with people at the margins of society;
+ touches people who have contagious and serious illnesses;
+ breaks well-regarded religious rules;
+ isn't especially interested in being the morality police;
+ speaks perpetually in puzzles called parables and only explains them to his closest friends;
+ preaches boldly against consumerism;
+ throws tables and gets upset at injustice;
+ is irritable – especially with his closest friends.

The Jesus of Mark's Gospel isn't palatable to the masses. In fact, he's such a threat to the status quo that he ends up crucified. This means that the Jesus we worship is more than our beloved Comforter. He is also a rebel, an outcast, a misunderstood healer, an advocate, a listener, a mysterious storyteller and a courageous contrarian.

Following Jesus means getting comfortable with all these layers. We don't get to pick and choose the qualities we like and don't like. Jesus is who he is regardless of whether we approve.

Jesus doesn't belong in a box and neither does anyone else. When we follow Jesus, we get to embrace him just as he is. May we offer ourselves and the rest of the world that same extension of grace.

The Gift List

Gift-giving and gift-receiving are two big themes at this time of year. Christmas lists are being exchanged. Presents are being wrapped. Cards are being mailed.

It's wonderful and joyful, and sometimes it's also stressful. We've now entered into that time of year when I start to feel anxious that I haven't given people enough gifts or I've given them the wrong gifts or I've forgotten someone altogether.

It's silly, I know. It's not the point of the season, I know. But it's an anxious emotional response that happens nevertheless.

As a way to prevent myself from sliding further into unnecessary worry and spending, I've decided to make a list. It's a gift list.

Only it isn't a list of gifts to purchase at the store. Instead, it's a list of gifts God has already given us. I'm hoping that by keeping this list handy, I'll be able to remain more centered in the true source of love at the center of all the seasonal jubilation.

In the Bible, Jesus often reflects on the gifts God has given. The New Testament was originally written in the Greek language, and the Greek word for "to give" is *didomi*. The Gospel of John uses the word *didomi* 63 times! John's list of the gifts our Creator gives to us includes:

+ Identity as a child of God (1:12)
+ Jesus (3:16)

- Holy Spirit (3:34 & 14:16)
- Eternal life (10:28)
- The example of Jesus (13:15)
- A new core commandment: "Love one another" (13:34)
- Peace (14:27)
- God's word (17:14)

Wow! What a list! John has recorded in his gospel the best gift list of all time. How miraculous and incredible that all those gifts are already available to us. We don't have to earn them or buy them or add them to our digital Amazon wish lists. These are treasures we already have through God's abundant grace.

Shortly before his death, Jesus prayed a long, powerful prayer. In that prayer, Jesus included the statement, "Now they [my disciples] know that everything you have given me comes from you." Jesus wanted his followers to recognize that everything good and important in life doesn't "poof" out of nowhere. It comes from God.

Jesus regularly talked about all of God's *didomi*-ing (giving) because he wanted people to recognize the Creator's abundant generosity. Jesus was always pointing back to God as the creative source of it all.

It's like Jesus took a string of Christmas lights and wrapped them around all the love and peace and goodness in creation - and then connected that string of lights to God, the origin of everything. For Jesus, that connection between God and everything else was a big deal. He hoped his followers might understand that we don't operate independently from God's presence and God's love.

We can certainly keep on making our lists and checking them twice, but maybe we can add another to the pile: the list of all the gifts we've already been given from our ever-creative, ever-loving, ever-generous God.

More than Muscles

He-Man shaped my earliest understanding of strength.

In the animated series, He-Man had big shoulders and chiseled features. He fought to keep Eternia safe from Skeletor and his nitwit henchmen. My childhood understanding of strength was defined by muscles too big for clothes and an arsenal of swords.

But that wasn't real strength. That was a cartoon, and He-Man and Skeletor were pretend.

"We need strength, not weakness." I've heard variations of this sentiment a lot lately from political candidates and commentators. Every time I hear the words strength and weakness used in discussions about leadership, I feel equal parts curious and concerned. Curious because I am fascinated by words and their meanings; concerned because I fear we are being served a plate of poison that, if ingested, may sicken us for decades.

It is time to have a collective conversation about strength and weakness. The world is presenting us with many options. Is strength authoritative or collaborative? Does strength bully to get its way, or does it compromise? Does a strong person forgive or hold a grudge? What takes more strength: admitting a mistake or assuming infallibility?

If it is true that we need strong leaders, then let us pause and consider the kind of strength we seek. The New Testament is a handy place to look for guidance on the topic.

The Greek word for strength is *dynatos*. According to the New Testament, a person with *dynatos* is mighty in influence and strong in soul.

Jesus has a particular penchant for using his strength to extend compassion for the oppressed, the downtrodden and the neglected. When they have no other hope, he shows up. He heals. He listens. He forgives.

It's worth noting that of all the things he could do with his strength, Jesus generally directs his power toward serving others. He empowers the disenfranchised. He listens to people who historically had no voice. He heals the folks that everyone else left at the city gate to die.

Even when other people resort to violence and the world seems to be ripping apart at the seams, Jesus refuses to subscribe to strength that expresses itself through domination and manipulation. He refuses to be that kind of leader. He never squishes people. Jesus uses his life to reveal a different kind of strength:

- strength that makes sure everyone gets a seat at the table.
- strength that brings the people at the back of the line to the front.
- strength that listens.

Jesus doesn't climb on people's backs to get to the top. He washes their feet - literally (see John 13).

Authentic strength isn't about muscles, wealth or prestige. Jesus forges a different path, and he invites us to do the same.

Good News?

The first chapter of the Gospel of Mark begins with the words, "The beginning of the good news of Jesus Christ, the Son of God." A few verses later, Jesus proclaims, "The time is fulfilled, and the kingdom of God has come near; repent, and believe in the good news."

So Jesus invites us to believe in the good news. Great. That sounds easy enough, right? Who doesn't like good news?

Generally, we associate good news with happy feelings. If someone arrives to a family gathering with good news to share, we assume they have some announcement which will be delightful for everyone.

The trouble is: Jesus' definition of good news is different than ours. So it can be confusing when Jesus says things that don't sound especially pleasant. He's not good on the small scale like coffee or snow days or a perfect slice of pie. Jesus is good in a way that stretches beyond our comprehension. His good news is like a community without access to fresh water receiving their first well or a war-torn land experiencing their first full day of peace.

Jesus' good news is transformative and deeply rooted, but to step into it we will often have to travel into uncomfortable, challenging territory. It is definitely a misreading of the Bible to assume Jesus wants us all to feel comfortable all the time.

However, it's easy to understand how many of us arrived at that incorrect assumption. For quite some time now, much of the Christian church, at least in this country, has equated following Jesus with being nice and agreeable. We've given into the temptation that being a good Christian means staying out of politics (or least never talking about it at church). We've avoided difficult conversations in favor of building community, however shallow it might be.

Most of this was unintentional. We thought we were doing the good, nice, pleasant thing. We believed that our tepid approach was safe and right.

But now we're paying a collective national price for the massive oversimplification of what it means to proclaim God's good news and follow Jesus.

So many people don't know what Jesus actually says about justice, helping the poor, consumerism, mercy and forgiveness. There are many Christians who don't know how fervently the prophets spoke against misuse of power. There are a lot of folks who deeply believe Jesus wants us to avoid conversations about what's happening in houses of government because it might cause a conflict in the church.

It is time for a change. Jesus' good news is not about everyone feeling happy all the time. We have the opportunity in this moment to learn how to disagree in healthy, life-giving ways - both inside and outside our congregations.

The good news of Jesus is not about everyone gaining wealth. It's not about the success of the market or the performance of our 401(k)s, and the gospel is certainly not about getting everyone to align with some moral code of behavior.

Instead, following Jesus into his good news story leads us into unexpected places. Sometimes the good news is like a nourishing balm. Sometimes it's a bitter pill that will heal us in the end. Following Jesus and hearing his good news sometimes leads us to rethink nearly everything about our lives, and that might leave us feeling uncertain about where we shop, how we vote, and what we do with our days.

Jesus' good news is the truth, and the truth sets us free. When we're willing to follow Jesus into his good news story no matter what the cost, everything becomes possible: change, healing, justice, forgiveness, and renewal.

People are hungry for depth. We long for the goodness of God in the deepest sense of the word - goodness that is rooted somewhere other than the sensation of another "like" on Facebook.

Jesus is good news in the flesh, and we get to spend our lives exploring what that means. What a glorious adventure!

Mystery upon Mystery

It is mystery upon mystery. It is eternity, grace, forgiveness, and community all wrapped in one. It is Holy Communion, Eucharist, and The Lord's Supper. This sacred meal is known by a variety of names and is celebrated with varying degrees of regularity across denominational lines.

It's possible you received the bread and wine/body and blood of Jesus within the last few days. Also possible: you have never experienced communion before or it has been a very long time.

Regardless of where you currently reside on the communion-receiving spectrum, Jesus accepts you and invites you to the table. These are just a couple of Jesus' core behavioral trademarks: acceptance and invitation.

Different denominations articulate the logistics of what takes place during the Lord's Supper in a variety of ways. But the truth is, no one church has the monopoly on eucharistic wisdom. Instead, denominations, congregations, and church leaders do their best to utilize the Bible and a strong dose of Holy Spirit guidance to make sense of something that is, at least in part, beyond human comprehension.

Here's what we know: Jesus started it. The idea for a meal involving both bread and wine that would correspond to body and blood came straight from our Savior himself. This meal was instituted by Jesus not long before he died; you can read three different accounts in Mark

14:12-26, Matthew 26:17-30, and Luke 22:7-23. Each version has its own unique slant on the meal details, but there are commonalities between all three.

With his closest friends around him, Jesus first took the bread. His words were: "This is my body given for you; do this in remembrance of me." This is almost identical to what most church leaders say during what is called the Words of Institution just before communion is served.

Of special note is the way Jesus described this bread/body as being "for you." It's for each of us, individually and communally.

Jesus then took a cup of wine. In Luke 22:20, Jesus said the wine was his blood, and it, too, was poured out "for you." Jesus was making it personal for the disciples. His words were a way of conveying to them that they mattered deeply.

When Jesus first said these words, he was still very much alive and hadn't yet been crucified. He also hadn't yet resurrected from the dead.

Nowadays, as we hear Jesus' words about the body and blood, sacrifice and forgiveness, we can understand that he was also giving his disciples a preview of what would soon be happening. Jesus wanted his friends to know that his death and resurrection were intimately tied to this holy meal. He wanted them to catch a glimpse of the reality that somehow, through a deep, unthinkable loss, there would be redemption and healing for all of creation.

When we experience communion, all these realities break into our everyday lives. Jesus breathes into us healing, forgiveness, connection, and hope. Not only are we reconnected with the risen Christ, we are reconnected to one another - ready to head back into the world with the knowledge that God walks with us.

Everyone feels a little different when they receive communion, and that's perfectly okay. Joy, tears, numbness, exuberance, confusion, happiness, gratitude, it's all completely appropriate. The presence of Jesus as experienced through the Lord's Supper has a way of filling our spirits with a host of emotions.

We don't earn Holy Communion and we're not expected to fully understand it. It's a gift. And as with all Jesus-style gifts, sometimes the best way to express our gratitude is to allow our often-heavy human hearts the opportunity to encounter the abundant, overflowing, never-fading love of Christ.

Graduates:
This One's for You

If Jesus went on a tour of the world, giving a commencement speech at each stop, I wonder what he'd say. Would he give advice? Would he read from the Bible? Would he feed the whole auditorium with a few loaves of bread and some fish?

Graduation is a sacred time of transition. This is true for every age at which a form of graduation ceremony exists, from preschool through a PhD. As I pondered what kind of wisdom Jesus might share with this year's graduates, a few ideas came to mind. These are all words of Jesus found within the Gospel of Matthew. Graduates: this one's for you.

"Do not judge, so that you may not be judged."

It is nearly impossible to go even an hour without making a judgment about another person. Jesus knew it was a challenging command. He also knew that an attitude of condemnation and judgment is completely toxic to you and everyone around you. When faced with an opportunity to judge another human being, spend your energy on something more productive. Like love. Speaking of which...

"Love God and love your neighbor. PS: Love your enemies and pray for those who persecute you."

Jesus believed that the two most important commandments were to love God and love others. But he didn't stop there. Jesus also commanded that we love people we don't even like. It's good advice that has stood up to the test of time. Throughout your life, you will no doubt meet people who make you mad, hurt you, and completely annoy you. Love them and pray for them. The whole world will be a more peaceful place when you are able to love the least lovable.

"The last will be first and the first will be last."

For high school and college graduates, you are likely feeling pressure to be the best. You need to get into the best school, to find the highest paying job, to find a new laptop with all the latest features. But whenever Jesus talked about eternity, he always surprised people by reminding them that life isn't about being the richest, most religious, or smartest. Instead, if you really want to achieve brilliance, be compassionate, forgiving, and generous.

"You are the light of the world."

If Jesus were sharing a commencement address today, I imagine he would certainly include these words. You are, indeed, a light to the world. No one can shine like you shine. You are important. You are valuable. And you are loved. Spread God's love everywhere you go, and shine, shine, shine.

Congratulations graduates. I hope that Jesus' words of love and guidance will be written on your hearts. May you always know that God is with you. And remember, nothing will ever separate you from Christ's love.

Changing Winds

Recent news reports on the local and international level have reminded me of a fascinating reality: Public opinion changes. Sometimes it happens quickly and sometimes very slowly - but people are fickle.

In 1879, when Thomas Edison patented the first light bulb available for home use, many people were afraid of electricity. To calm those fears, the light bulbs came with a warning: *Do not attempt to light with a match. The use of electricity is in no way harmful to health, nor does it affect the soundness of your sleep.* Nowadays, most households are reliant on electricity in a variety of forms - all day, every day - and the fear that once existed no longer does. Public opinion changed.

In the nineteenth century, a good chunk of the population didn't think women should vote. Over time, however, public opinion changed and thankfully, as of 1920, there is no gender restriction on Election Day.

In 1917, the USDA Food Pyramid was originally released to the public. It has since undergone a variety of changes. Butter and margarine actually had their own food group in the 1930s! We've all seen the shifting tides of public opinion when it comes to diet. High fat, low fat, no carb, high carb. Public opinion changes.

We see it in our opinions about celebrities, newscasters, neighbors, and even our own families. We love them until they do something we don't like - perhaps something that reminds us of our own shortcomings - and then our opinions shift. We not only don't like them, sometimes we even shun them.

Jesus faced these challenges in his ministry, too. In the sixth chapter of the Gospel of Mark, Jesus enters his hometown to teach and preach. Initially, everyone is astounded.

But then, the crowd changes their tone. The winds shift. They say something like, "But this kid is the son of Mary! We know his brothers. We know his sisters." They don't mention a father, perhaps a hint that his paternity is questioned in town. The Gospel mentions that they take offense at him. The Greek word is *skandalidzo* - from which we get our English word "scandalize." Public opinion changed in the blink of an eye.

But Jesus keeps going. He keeps teaching and healing. Jesus perseveres. He gets ahold of the disciples and the journey continues. Two by two he sends them out to bring a message of repentance and healing. Jesus tells them to keep going and not get discouraged regardless of how they are received.

Jesus encourages us to take a similar approach: to live and share the Gospel, the good news of Jesus' love and forgiveness, regardless of outside circumstances, regardless of public opinion, regardless of trends, regardless of moods (our own or someone else's). We're called to shake off what doesn't work - and keep going. Persevere. Love. Share.

Disappointments happen - they just do - in life, in work, and in church. But Jesus reminds us to keep going. Even when the disappointments are large and it feels like the world is against us, keep going.

Jesus' model of perseverance despite public opinion is a helpful one for us all. We all face the temptation to seek approval. I would imagine there were times when Jesus felt it, too. We all long to know we are valued and liked and appreciated. Sometimes we base our decisions and behaviors on whether or not we'll be in the good graces of others. But Jesus reminds us to rethink this tendency because the bottom line is that the opinions of others are not consistent. They change, sometimes like the wind.

But the mission to which we are called doesn't change. Love, serve, heal, forgive - no matter what. Follow Jesus - no matter what. May we find courage along the way, regardless of where the changing winds of public opinion might blow.

Nature

Training a
Female Pheasant

I was on my lunch break the first time I saw her. I glanced out the dining room window, and there she was, nestled between some dirt and snow in the field. Her color was a soft brown, like caramel, and she had a dark ring around her eye.

"That's one of the loveliest birds I've ever seen," I thought. Wanting to remember her forever, I ran to get my camera. I put on my boots and coat and ran outside to take some photos. I was not particularly quiet or graceful in my opening of the back door, so when the bird heard me, she stood up and started running.

"No, no, Lady! I just want to take your picture," I yelled. She kept running, but I did snap a quick photo. It was then that I named her Lady.

My bird identification skills leave a lot to be desired, so I posted Lady's photo on Facebook. A bunch of friends responded right away with her species: a pheasant.

The next day I saw Lady again. She was in the field in nearly the same spot, looking very intent, like she was thinking about some internal struggle going on in her bird family. I didn't chase her down for a photo that day. I just admired her from afar.

But I did start worrying about her. Where does she get her food? If I brought her snack, what would she like? How does she stay warm? What if someone tries to shoot her?

It was a few days before I saw my feathered friend again wandering around the yard. I was in my car on the way to work, and I was very glad to see her. "I wonder if I can train Lady?" I thought to myself.

That night when I got home, I Googled, *Training a female pheasant.* There were zero hits! Can you believe that? I didn't even know it was possible to Google something and not get any responses. I guess it means you really can't train pheasants.

It's been over a week since I've seen Lady. She probably found a new yard to sit in. Or maybe she discovered a home a little farther from the road. I would actually be glad if that were the case, because I was afraid she might get injured.

It sure was fun to see her a few times, and I'd be happy to spot her again. But sometimes we just have to appreciate a gift for what it is. We can't make good things last forever. Whether it's a perfect meal or a great vacation or a meaningful conversation, many of life's most wonderful blessings are best when they are valued right in the moment.

It is most likely I won't see Lady again. Nevertheless, I'll continue looking. There is beauty all around us all the time, and I'm thankful for the bird that reminded me to always keep my eyes peeled.

Holy Truths

At some point along the way, I unknowingly signed up for a lifelong course in "Holy Truths." These informal classes most often take place where the sky above serves as the only roof.

God teaches these classes most often when I'm not looking. The lessons show up like shooting stars, unpredictable and swift. They are moments that can't be saved but only savored.

On a recent afternoon at Gooseberry Falls along the North Shore of Lake Superior, two flowers seemed to call out and say: "Look over here. Listen and learn."

Does every flower come with some analogous lesson? Does nature conspire together to teach human beings holy truths?

Maybe so - but probably not. Nature is too wise for conspiracies. Creation continues with or without our observations and speculations. The holy truths discovered outdoors seem most profound precisely because plants, trees, animals are unrehearsed. They are honest and unfiltered.

At Gooseberry Falls, the yellow flower caught my attention first. She stood straight up to the sky. There were no other flowers in her midst. At some point this spring she took root in an unlikely spot: surrounded by tall pines digesting most of her light. But the lack of sunshine didn't stop this little flower. She stretched and stretched until she found a spot where the sun's rays broke through the trees.

It was a vivid reminder to me of the reality that sometimes we have to stretch a lot farther than we'd prefer to stretch. Situations arise that leave us in the shade, and we have to find another way to get a regular dose of light and hope. There are occasions in which we have to emotionally and physically push ourselves until we're even a bit sore. But it's worth it because in the end, we are able to stand tall and soak in those longed-for rays of encouragement.

Next was the purple flower residing near the falls. I believe it was a violet, but I wouldn't call my identification skills particularly strong. If it was a violet, this one was absolutely not of the shrinking variety. He was brave. Of all the places for a violet to grow, this particular specimen chose to cling sideways from a small crevice on a rock.

To a novice observer like myself, the growing conditions seemed less than ideal. What about good soil? And enough light? Could this little violet receive all its needed nourishment from the side of a rock?

Apparently yes, as this precious purple plant was making the best of it and blooming where he was planted.

I have an affinity for the word bloom. It's plastered in my bedroom on the wall as removable word art. There are calendars and photo frames sporting the word as well. I know the saying is so familiar it's cliche: "Bloom wherever you're planted." But it makes sense.

In our own lives, sometimes we, like the violet at Gooseberry Falls, have to bloom where we are planted. The situations we find ourselves in may not be perfect, but we can seek out and lean on the support of others. We can pursue opportunities to nourish our spirits, and - even when it feels unlikely - we can continue to grow.

A vacation hike at Gooseberry Falls ended up providing the space for a sacred classroom. What a gift it is to worship a God who comes to us in such a multitude of ways.

Being Superior

Vast and mysterious. Relentlessly captivating. Each visit to Lake Superior reveals another angle from which to experience awe. Every encounter with the giant lake has changed me.

She reminds me of what matters and what doesn't. Her mesmerizing presence siphons out all the unsettled, ridiculous, anxiety-ridden clutter in my mind until all that remains is peace.

Every morning Lake Superior offers up her truest self. I like that. She doesn't ask for feedback. She doesn't check in with all the local travelers to see how they'd like her to behave. No one gets to make requests.

Instead, Lake Superior just is. Her waves unfurl. Giant, splashing hills of water morph overnight into a glassy stillness. It happens just like that. I stand amazed. Witnessing such authenticity feels like a permission slip. Be a sky full of ominous clouds. Be sunshine and surprise. Be a tempestuous storm. Be however, whatever, whoever you are.

On the first full day of a recent North Shore vacation, I announced to my mom, Pam, and my fiancé, Justin, "I have one goal for today. I want to touch the Gitchi-Gami." That's the original name the Ojibway gave to Lake Superior; there are many alternative spellings. It means "huge water," and it is. Over all the earth, it is the largest of the freshwater lakes.

A woman with a car covered in eclectic stickers told us where to find the nearest public beach. "Two miles up the road. There's no sand, just rocks. It's right across from Isak Hansen True Value."

There was no one else there when we arrived. The shoreline beckoned. The three of us spread out across the piles of eons-old rocks, each taking in the wonder. I stepped to the edge of a large, flat stone and dipped in the tops of my fingers. Cold. Alive.

Each time I touch the Gitchi-Gami, it is a rebirth, a baptism, a reminder of my actual identity. Touching the waters of Lake Superior is a sensory experience of an eternal truth woven into the fibers of everything. We're connected: to the earth, to one another, to the whole creation, to the lava that formed the lake's basin, to the lichen covering the boulders at Cascade River State Park, to the Romanian server at Papa Charlie's spending his first summer in the United States. The waters connect us all.

What color is the lake? Ever-changing. Sometimes it is light gray with a horizon line that darts across the sky like thick charcoal. Then the next morning, it is royal blue with caps of white. There also are times of nothing but colorless fog and mist.

Lake Superior is a force, strong and persistent. The Gitchi-Gami is a sage, profoundly wise and eager to teach. Beside her waters, I am a speechless student ready to learn. She whispers, "Be. Just be."

Lady Returns

You're not going to believe who I saw last week. Lady! Lady the Pheasant! She was in my backyard again.

Earlier this winter, Lady brought delight to my heart several times as I observed her out in the field. After that, I didn't see her again. I imagined her having a pleasant pheasant winter in a nice cozy spot with her bird friends.

Then, last week, something amazing happened. I was home for lunch, attempting to bounce back from a challenging day. I'm certain you've had those days, too.

When I am feeling overwhelmed, I find it helps to take a small break and refocus. As I was eating some pineapple to gladden my heart, I happened to look out the window. At the edge of the tree line I could make out something beige-colored, but it was well beyond what I could clearly see. To my overactive imagination, I pondered whether it might be a mountain lion or a fox!

I reached for the binoculars. "IT'S LADY!" I squealed. Tears of delight immediately welled up in my eyes.

I don't know what it is about this bird, but she brings me such joy! After taking a few photos of her and dancing around my living room, I realized something had happened inside. I wasn't sad or mad or frustrated anymore. I felt peaceful and filled with joy. Gratitude filled up all my cells at the mere sight of a beautiful bird sitting on a pile of snow.

I rejoiced.

Today's Lenten column features a single verse, Psalm 118:24. It states, "This is the day that the Lord has made. Let us rejoice and be glad in it." It's a great reminder to be joyful and trust that every day is a new, God-filled day.

Truth be told, sometimes we don't feel like rejoicing. Sometimes we feel like pouting and complaining. Sometimes we want to stay in our beds and watch episodes of *Days of our Lives* for weeks on end. But God wants more for us. God wants joy and abundance for our spirits.

There are reasons to rejoice all around us. They come in all shapes and sizes. The friendly stranger at the library. A sale on refried beans. The sight of violinists and their bouncing bows at the symphony. A new quilting pattern from a friend. An opportunity to collect cans for a local food pantry. A heartwarming conversation after a funeral. The sound of your friends singing karaoke.

This IS the day that the Lord has made. This very day. So rejoice! Be glad! Today is a once-in-a-lifetime opportunity.

The Aisle of Seeds

In the middle of December, when summer was a far-off figment of my frozen imagination, taking care of my own garden seemed like something that would be a source of endless fun. As one who spent the past decade renting, I had little sense for the actual work involved.

Reality check! Gardens are a lot of work! Good work, I have come to realize, but work nevertheless.

Last month, when the weeds in the plot I inherited started coming in, I panicked. I worried that I wasn't going to have time for a garden. Admittedly, it was a particularly busy time at work, and when I am busy, I am also highly irrational. I texted my fiancé, Justin, who lives in Cedar Rapids.

"I've got to do something about the garden! It's full of weeds and looks hideous! What if the neighbors hate the sight of it? Maybe I should just cover it up! I don't think I'll have time to landscape, mow, and take care of the garden. I'm going to Fleet Farm."

The mission was clear: Avoid weeding at all costs and cover up the garden!

Fleet Farm is like my own personal version of the board game, Settlers of Catan. I don't get it but I wish I did, and until I do, I'll just pretend. I don't go to Fleet Farm often enough to be familiar with the layout of the store, so a "quick trip" ends up taking an hour.

Another text to Justin, "I think I'll just get a giant tarp!"

Justin's response, "I don't think that's a great idea, Em. The tarp will grow mold. And what if we want to plant things there later this spring or summer? What about using some hay? Or garden fabric."

Me: "No, no! This tarp says, 'Mold-free.' I'm getting the tarp and I'm just going to cover it all up. Talk to you later!"

An hour later, I had traded the giant brown tarp for some garden fabric but it still didn't feel quite right. I was making a garden mole hill into an insurmountable mountain. It was just a little plot of dirt that needed to be weeded, for crying out loud.

It was at that moment that I stumbled into the aisle of seeds. Seeds upon seeds. Flowers. Vegetables. Herbs. Everyone in that aisle seemed happy and capable of weeding, which made me feel like I could be capable of weeding, too. The solution was clear: weed the garden and then grow the seeds.

Text to Justin: "Change of plans! I'm going to just go ahead and weed the garden. I don't know what I was thinking. I'm really irrational when I'm tired and busy."

And so began a new chapter in my relationship with weeds. Crab grass, bull thistle, creeping Charlie, dandelions, they aren't really so bad after all (their resilience and determination is inspiring!). With gloves and the proper tools, weeds come out of the soil just fine, and the act of pulling them is surprisingly gratifying.

In the end, the garden was weeded. Last Saturday, Justin was in town and we planted tomatoes, peppers, beets, and radishes. I'm looking forward to homemade salsa later this summer!

So often it is tempting to avoid what we perceive to be difficult in our lives. We imagine it would be easier to just ignore our problems, wounds, and frustrations or cover them all up with a giant tarp. When we do that, we miss out on a lot of beautiful possibilities. Advice from a novice gardener: skip the tarp and do the work. Weed the garden. Then grow some seeds.

Seasonally Yours

D earest Winter,

We meet again, old friend. You, with your slippery parking lots and arctic wind chills. Me, with my inability to remember to wear gloves and a hat. I'm writing to share some exciting news.

Usually, I start to pine away for your cousin, Spring, the first evening that dips below 40 degrees. But something new is happening between us, Winter. You're capturing a tiny slice of my seasonally frozen heart.

I never thought I'd say this, but there is something very nearly nice about you. I've worn my boots a few times, and that's been swell. And my mom let me borrow a pair of her amazing thermal socks, which made for delightfully warm toes! I've enjoyed the gorgeous colors of the sun rising and setting. The feel of crisp, cool air in my lungs has been practically refreshing.

Some people really, really appreciate you. I'm thankful for those folks, too. They spend all year looking forward to activities like ice fishing, snowmobiling and skiing. It's heart-warming to see how much they love the snow and even the cold. As much I prefer sweating in the warm sun, it has been good for me to remember how much your presence means to others. You've got quite a fan club, Winter-time.

You are a season that fortifies us. It's a time of year to be strengthened and renewed under a giant pile of blankets. It's a season to sit beside a roaring fire and savor every drop of a hot beverage. You give us the opportunity to pause and reflect.

There's a song in one of my grandma's old piano books that I like to play sometimes. It's called "I Don't Know Why (I Just Do)." It was popular in the 1930s, the 1940s and again in the 1960s.

These are my favorite lyrics:

I don't know why I love you like I do.
I don't know why, I just do.
I don't know why you thrill me like you do.
I don't know why, you just do.

That's how I feel about you, dear Winter. I never thought I'd like you, but I guess I just do.

So thank you. Thank you for expanding my seasonal preferences. I still look forward to seeing Cousin Spring very soon, but in the meantime, please know that you, too, are appreciated.

As the writer of the biblical book of Ecclesiastes wrote long ago, "There is a time for everything, and a season for every activity under heaven." And you, my darling Winter, are certainly a special piece of the puzzle.

I apologize for not writing sooner. Please do stay in touch.

Seasonally yours,

Emily

Seasonal Magic

Spring took its precious time arriving this year. Cold temperatures and April snowstorms left many of us feeling exhausted and a bit crabby. Our collective waiting for warmth began to feel like watching a pot of water that just wouldn't boil.

But then, as if by some glorious seasonal magic trick, the temperatures increased and the sun returned. I've never seen the people of the Med City so happy. It's amazing what a stretch of 60-degree days will do for folks who haven't encountered such temperatures in many a moon.

The shift feels so novel and new. I've never taken so many photos of grass. Just plain ol' patches of green spindly growth. Anything poking up through the brown, crunchy leaves gets its own snapshot and a whispered prayer, "Dear God, I forgot that grass is beautiful. How could I ever imagine it an annoyance? It's a miracle!"

Soon enough the leaves on the trees will fill in and the landscape will transition into its lush, summery state. That, too, will be lovely, but I'm not in a hurry. This stretch of time in-between carries its own splendor.

During a recent trip to Whitewater State Park, there were examples of the magnificent seasonal in-between everywhere. Tiny ferns were beginning to unfurl little arms. A few early Dutchman's breeches were hanging out to dry. There were all sorts of emerging ephemerals and birds in a perpetual state of song.

The novelty of all the sights and sounds reminded me of a verse from the Old Testament book of Isaiah. In Isaiah 43:19a, God says, "Watch for the new thing I am going to do. It is happening already - you can see it now!" (Good News Translation).

Another translation of the same verse describes God as a kind of gardener: "I am doing something new! Now you will grow like a new plant. Surely you know this is true," (Easy to Read Version).

Spring feels like a very new thing this year. According to the calendar, it's a season that comes every nine months, but somehow it still feels like a marvelous surprise. Maybe that's one of the mercies of living in a place with four different seasons. Each one has its own unique beauty.

One of my favorite sights during the Whitewater trip was the sight of a hepatica flower just about to open. A solitary stem slowly stretched upward toward the midday sun. "How long has this sweet plant been waiting for this moment?" I wondered. From seed to dirt to life above ground, it took patience and resilience.

We are all that little hepatica flower at times: waiting and wondering, hoping for a change in seasons, longing for warmth and the nutrients we need to transform and stretch out our leaves, and delighting in the miraculous, mysterious timing of it all.

Thanks be to God for this season of growth, for tiny signs of hope, and for all the new things God is doing in our midst.

A Delicious Discovery

What do skunk cabbage, trout lily, trillium, and dutchman's breeches have in common? I'll give you a hint; they are not song titles of an obscure 1980s album by Metallica. Nor are they pet names for my boyfriend. Instead, they are all variations of spring ephemerals.

I learned about ephemerals with my mom during a recent tour at the Eloise Butler Wildflower Garden and Bird Sanctuary in Minneapolis. It's a wonderful, historic, free-of-charge park in the middle of the city.

Ephemerals are wildflowers that grow in early spring. They bloom quickly and then their flowers and leaves wither back into the ground. True ephemerals go through their entire growth cycle before the leaves are fully formed on the trees that tower above them. Some ephemerals, like twinleaf (Latin name: *Jeffersonia diphylla*), only bloom for a total of two days! Don't blink or you might miss their beautiful white petals!

The reason these special flowers bloom and then wither so quickly is because their access to sunlight is drastically impaired when leaves on the surrounding trees develop. Flowers like twinleaf and trout lily take advantage of the bare tree branches of early spring and soak up all the light they can. By the time summer rolls around, the early wildflowers are gone and the gluttonous deciduous trees can gobble up all the light they want.

Our tour guide at Eloise Butler was Kyla. An expert in weaving together history, herbalism, and botany, Kyla talked about ephemerals in a way that made the entire forest come alive before our eyes. I always assumed early spring was a boring part of the growing season in Minnesota. I was wrong! The woods are utterly alive and enticing in early spring. It is a precious, swiftly moving season - and one that reveals delicate petals and stems much too sweet to miss.

The garden tour revealed that ephemerals are teachers. They are like the wise sage instructing her students to sit quietly and observe. One must kneel or squat to visit these seasonal friends. In the midst of a societal pace that can so often feel rushed and frenetic, ephemerals whisper, "Come here. Slow down. Look."

Ephemerals are graceful reminders: the beautiful, wonderful parts of life are sometimes fleeting, but this doesn't make them any less splendid or worthy-of-note. There are seasons and rhythms to everything, even the daintiest flowers of the forest floor. We can't make time stand still, but we can slow down and be present. We can stop and soak in whatever beauty is around us — the way the cream swirls in the coffee, the couple standing in line holding hands, those stubborn weeds that refuse to stop growing in the cracks of the driveway. These details are found in life's fleeting moments, and they are a divine gift.

After nearly eight years in this great state, each season continues to reveal new surprises. The ephemerals are a delicious discovery, and one I will now savor every spring.

The Whispering Desert

The desert doesn't yell. It whispers.

The region around Tucson, Arizona, doesn't loudly boast its wisdom. It doesn't brag about its profound resilience and ecological interconnectedness. Instead, the desert humbly invites visitors to come close, listen and observe.

I had the opportunity to answer this call a few weeks ago when Justin and I went to Arizona for our belated honeymoon. It was a landscape unlike any I'd ever experienced.

An abundance of cacti dotted the terrain: prickly pear, saguaro, jumping cholla, and teddy bear cholla. I had no idea there were so many kinds of cacti. All I'd ever taken the time to learn about them was that they were covered in needles and could store large amounts of water.

Little did I know the critical role cacti play in the desert ecosystem. They are home to all kinds of birds, mammals, and insects. The fruit of several cactus varieties in the region are edible to humans and have been staples in the diets of many Native American communities for thousands of years.

Not all deserts are created equal; they vary immensely. The desert region near Tucson is called the Sonoran Desert. It stretches into parts of Mexico and California. Part of this desert's beauty stems from the amazing things it can do with only 12 inches of rain per year. Rochester, by comparison, gets about 34 inches of rain per year and 49 inches of snow.

Measurable precipitation happens only about 30 days per year in Tucson. We happened to be there on a rainy day. Everyone we encountered was overjoyed about it. "It hasn't rained here in eight months," they all said. "We really needed this rain."

Despite the downpour, Justin and I made our way to the visitors center. We watched as water dumped down from the sky and cars splashed through giant pools in the streets.

While the rain delayed our outdoor activities, it led us to a much deeper appreciation for how much water matters in the desert. By the time we got out on a hike, we saw its impact immediately.

There's a type of flora in the Sonoran Desert that's often called by its nickname, resurrection plant. It can go for very long periods without any water at all. It appears dry and dead. But then, within moments of getting any hydration, it becomes almost neon in color and its tiny leaves become lush and full. Its transformation was a mesmerizing example of what it looks like to bounce back - a floral resurrection.

Later, on a guided horse ride, we met an avian friend: a red-tailed hawk. The leader of our trail ride noticed it perched atop a tall saguaro cactus. The dignified raptor stayed in the very same spot for nearly an hour. Perhaps she was waiting for some supper, or maybe she was just gifting us with an extended viewing of her majesty. Whatever her intention, the hawk was patience in a feathered body.

At Saguaro National Park, we observed ancient petroglyphs. No one knows for certain what the symbols mean. They were a fabulous curiosity to observe. Hundreds of years ago the images were engraved by real people with real hands. They were emojis of yesteryear. The petroglyphs served as a kind of bridge connecting us to another time and place altogether.

From the Gambel's quail to the howling coyotes to Orion shining brightly in the sky, the trip was a beautiful mystery to behold. I hope someday we can go back and listen to the desert whisper once more.

Tiny Eternity

God's peace shined upon my spirit in the mountains of North Carolina.

Earlier this month, Justin and I traveled there for the wedding of dear friends. We savored time with the wedding crew and then explored the city of Asheville for a couple days. After that, we headed out to the mountains near Pisgah National Forest and Great Smoky Mountain National Park.

The trip was a dream come true, and we both found ourselves enamored by the weather, culture, history and landscape of the region.

A special highlight for me was the time we spent in the mountains near Hot Springs. We stayed in a small cabin that backed up to 100 acres of forest. The land was available to cabin guests for hiking and exploration and included a waterfall, mineral spring, two labyrinths, a whimsical "Mermaid Lodge," and an immense array of walkable trails. The lush greenery and fresh, higher-altitude air were refreshing.

Heavy rains passed through while we were at the cabin and lasted for a day. A few hours after the storm passed, we headed out for a hike.

Just over an hour into the expedition, we walked through an open field of tall grass. As we re-entered the wooded forest, I looked up to see blue sky peering through the clouds. A few moments after that, the brilliant sun broke through for about a minute. Without a conscious thought, I reflexively turned toward the sun and stretched my arms wide as I stood in the rays. In those moments, I experienced a tiny, mysterious eternity - a stretch of time packed with limitless bliss and a sense of immense gratitude. I felt free and peaceful, connected and aware.

Unbeknownst to me, Justin was standing behind me at the time, and he captured the moment on his cell phone camera. I'm thankful to have photographic evidence of such a brief, impactful experience.

God's radiant peace, love, and glory often shine into life unexpectedly. When those special occasions arise, what more can we do but turn toward them with open arms ready to revel in the wonder?

Many worship services conclude with a final blessing that's something along the lines of: "May the Lord bless and keep you, may the Lord's face shine on you and be gracious to you, may the Lord look upon you with favor and give you peace" (a variation of Numbers 4:24-26).

Those familiar words now have an added layer of meaning for me. As the sun peeked through the clouds on a mountain on the North Carolina/Tennessee border, I felt a glimpse of the face of a loving Creator shining upon the world. It was a powerful physical experience of a blessing I've heard recited hundreds of times.

I will be on the lookout for more tiny eternities, and when they occur, I pray for the awareness to turn toward them with an open heart and arms stretched wide.

Pause

Breathing Break

We are brilliant fiction writers. Whether or not we ever put words to an actual page, we're writing stories all day every day in our minds without even realizing it. This is a good news, bad news situation.

The good news: Our ability to create fictional stories about everyone and everything is a wonder of the human mind. We can use our imaginations to do good in the world: to solve problems, entertain, and empathize.

The bad news: Much of the time, the fictional stories we write are incomplete at best and harmful at worst. These stories we write can lead us astray in our relationships, which can lead to ample suffering. They can also nudge us toward making lots of false judgments.

I've just completed a six-week "Introduction to Meditation" class at the Rochester Meditation Center. The course has been one of the more impactful learning experiences of my life, and that is not an exaggeration. Especially helpful is how the course has empowered me to develop a new, healthier relationship with what's happening in my cranium from the moment I wake up until the moment I go to sleep.

All day long, our brains keep us occupied with thoughts and feelings. These thoughts and feelings are not inherently bad, but they do tend to be all-consuming. They are based on our individual perceptions of reality, and we use them to write stories and draw conclusions.

We're always filling in the blanks of our stories with our imaginations. It's a mostly unconscious process until we become aware of it. Human beings have a bonus feature called consciousness that enables us to notice our thoughts and feelings taking place. Awareness enables us to recognize that we are so much more than what we think and feel in any given moment.

When we interact with another person, our brains often try to put labels and judgments on the experience. They aren't always negative, but sometimes they are. We learn about a person's religion or job or political affiliation, and then our brains set about creatively filling in the rest of the blanks. Or someone interacts with us in a way we find unsettling, and we immediately write the story of why it happened and how awful the other person is for being such a bonehead.

If left in unawareness, we tend to categorize everything and everyone. Again, it's mostly an unconscious process. Nice. Mean. Loud. Bossy. Rude. Good. Bad. Naive. Extreme. Awful. Wealthy. Poor. Positive. Negative. Young. Old. Straight. Gay. Our thoughts will go on writing a fictional story about everyone we meet and everything we experience.

We all know the feeling of making a snap judgement about some person or event and then later discovering we were totally wrong. This happens to all of us (regularly)! It's an opportunity to practice awareness. When we're able to suspend the need to write stories and make judgments, then we're making real progress.

It takes an intentional slowing down of these automatic fiction-writing processes in order to live a more conscious, compassionate life. One way to do this is to take intentional breathing breaks in which we stop what we're doing and breathe deeply with awareness.

The truth is that we never know as much as we think we know about anything or anyone. We tend to write all kinds of stories about people's motivations, attitudes and choices, but we do it without ever knowing the totality of the lived experiences of those people. Usually we know a sliver of a sliver of a sliver of the story of another person; it's a total waste of time to draw any judgments or write any stories based on such a small piece of the pie.

I fiercely believe the world needs more of us to commit to tapping into our collective loving kindness. May we all have the courage to step away from our fictional stories and toward a life of compassionate awareness.

Window Washing

Cleaning the windows can be a spiritually enlightening task.

Some chores are fun. Others are less so. Household tasks I consistently find enjoyable: laundry, vacuuming, and cooking different varieties of beans.

Not so with windows. Until very recently, I've avoided window-washing at all costs. It always seemed so tedious. It was also a task that appeared inconsequential; would it really make a difference if they were regularly cleaned? If not, why bother?

A year has passed since I moved from Stewartville into Rochester. The windows made it a full circle around the sun without a cleaning.

Then, one Sunday afternoon, I passed through the kitchen to make a cup of tea. While it was perfectly sunny outside, the dirty windows made it appear hazy and overcast inside. There was only one way to remedy the situation.

"The time has come," I proclaimed. "The windows of this house need a scrub."

During the process, I learned something all of you probably already know: Cleaning the windows actually makes a huge difference in the overall brightness of a room. How this important life lesson was missed is unclear.

What I find most surprising is that I had no idea how dirty the windows were until after they had been cleaned. A clearer view was possible the entire time but I hadn't taken the steps to make that possibility into reality. Once the windows were washed, the new perspective was refreshing.

Inner Windows

This weekend I turn 35. My friend commiserated the other day, "Don't you feel like we're getting so old?"

"Not really!" I replied. "Mostly I just feel like I'm finally figuring some things out."

I feel like my inner windows are finally getting clean - like I finally have the tools to do the task.

Until these last few years, I had no idea how much judgments, fears and insecurities were blocking my view of reality. Thoughts and feelings ran the show. All too often, the world appeared to be a fearful place full of potential disappointments. Instead of attending to the layers of crud piling up on my spirit's window, I pretended everything was fine.

You can guess how well that worked.

Divine Wisdom has been revealing important truths over the last few years. Meditation, prayer, good rest and other awareness-building practices have become for me like a bucket of warm, eco-friendly soap and water. They help me keep a clear perspective of reality unencumbered with toxic states of mind that skew the view.

The clearer view has revealed a reality that has been there all along: Love is shining everywhere and all the time. Gratitude and peace are always possible.

How might you clear away some resentment and judgment from your inner window this summer? What practices help you boost your capacity to view your own reflection with compassion and to look upon your neighbor with love?

Spend time doing those practices. Taking opportunities to attend to our inner spiritual windows will always be a good investment of energy. You may be surprised at just how much of a difference it can make.

Electronic
Overwhelm

These days, email is everywhere. It is estimated that there are five billion active email accounts in existence. The average employee spends somewhere around four hours of each eight-hour workday responding to email, and our inbox time isn't limited to our jobs. Many of us also maintain personal email accounts.

Yet even as the use of email has risen, most of us haven't ever had any training in how to use it most impactfully. "Electronic overwhelm" is a common occurrence for many. We wonder: How do we prioritize the contents of our inboxes? How much time should we spend on it each day? How can we electronically express our feelings without being misunderstood?

Thankfully, overwhelm isn't the only possible way to deal with email. We can also try mindfulness.

Mindfulness is an approach to life that is rooted in an awareness of the present moment. Here are a few suggestions for how to embrace a mindful approach to email:

+ **Breathe.** Start your workday with your breath. Before you type in the password to log into your inbox, sit at your desk with both shoes touching the floor. Breathe in and out slowly and consciously. Feel the air tickling your nose hairs.

If you pray, this would be a great moment to pray for guidance for the day ahead. Consider setting an intention for how you'd like to feel as you spend time in your inbox that day. Return to your breath and then log in.

The whole exercise could last as little as a minute, but a single minute spent wisely can set the mood for the day.

* **Practice gratitude.** Sometimes when I'm digging out from an email avalanche at work, I notice that I begin to feel a little bitter. I think, "Ufff! I didn't get into this job because I wanted to spend all this time on email. I want to be talking to actual people and doing meaningful work."

But what if email is part of meaningful work? What if email can be a tool for building stronger workplaces and relationships? It's useful to stop now and then and think of reasons why email is a source of thankfulness. It connects us to others. It can be archived easily. It can be a quick way to convey information. What aspects of email do you find gratitude-worthy?

* **Respond don't react.** An effective way to start despising your email account is by getting into a pattern of reacting instead of responding. When you read an email that triggers an emotional response, that's a good moment to pause and tune into the feeling.

Before writing another word, stop and listen to yourself. Has reading the email brought up feelings of defensiveness? Anger? Bliss? Confusion? Notice that it's not so much the content of the email that's creating the emotions. Instead, it's you reacting to the email's contents.

As often as possible in life (whether digitally or in person), we want to avoid communicating out of a place of reactivity. Instead, we want to first process our feelings so we can witness reality more clearly. We can then respond in a more intentional, thoughtful way.

Email reactivity often leads to a long chain of passive-aggressive correspondence with all kinds of inappropriate cc-ing and bcc-ing. We've all been there; it's not pleasant.

* **Take breaks and be intentional.** Email is a great tool and a bad boss. Instead of fixating on cleaning out your email and keeping zero new messages in your inbox at all times, try creating more spacious-

ness. What might it look like to carve out a couple blocks a day to respond and craft emails and keep it off the rest of the day? In some cases that may not be practical but in others, it may work.

Remember that email doesn't need to feel like an endless marathon. Take breaks. Stay hydrated. Balance responding to emails with the rest of your vocational priorities.

Technology will continue to develop and more streamlined electronic communications approaches are certainly on the horizon. But for the foreseeable future, the use of email in the workplace isn't going anywhere. With a mindful approach, email can remain a fruitful, meaningful way of communicating.

The First Frost

The first frost left me feeling unexpectedly forlorn. This is Minnesota after all, and I've spent my whole life in the Midwest. The change in seasons is not a surprise.

And yet, the end of this particular growing season was hard. I wasn't ready to say goodbye to the ever-flowering banana pepper plants or the mums hanging in their baskets or the marigolds in their pots on the back deck.

Regardless of my readiness, the first snow fell and the plants froze, and it was time to say farewell.

On a dreary Saturday, Justin and I emptied out all the potted plants, separating the soil back into the garden and the plant matter into the pile of yard waste. We pulled the tomato cages out of the ground and tore down the remaining squash vines. Much was composted. Several plants (and even two small trees) were moved indoors. We filled in the garden holes that Finn, our dog, dug on hot summer days when he wanted some cool earth against his belly.

Had it really been six months since the garden began? That half-year felt like a nourishing inhale, a time to absorb all the oxygen-rich possibility. I thought of the multitude of dinners with friends on the porch, Justin perfecting his grilled salmon, so many post-work evenings of tortilla chips with hummus. It was beautiful.

Even dear Finn whimpered while we prepared the garden and yard for hibernation. I suppose he will miss having as much time in the backyard to get acquainted with his new friends through the fence. Perhaps he was also sad that the sun now goes to bed so early and he has less time to play refuse-to-fetch.

If the growing season was our collective inhale, then we are now headed into the great Minnesota exhale. The cold months. The time in which the soil takes a long nap and the furry creatures hibernate.

Last January when my mom, Pam, and I traveled to Kolkata, India, for Josh and Sweta's wedding, there was a refrain we heard throughout the four days. "Be sure to take rest," the gracious aunties and uncles would say. "Have you taken enough rest today?" the thoughtful cousins would ask.

In the midst of all the excitement and ceremonies, there was the reminder that rest was important. And now back home we enjoy the beauty of this frozen season and its uniquely special offerings. We give our yards and dirt and schedules breathing space, and we remember that rest is a good and necessary component of life.

This year Justin and I are trying something new. We're saving some seeds from each of our garden crops. Maybe it will work and another generation of garden will spring forth from this year's harvest. Or maybe it will be a small way to hold onto the nostalgia of our first garden in our first home.

"We better be sure to save the seeds of one of our squash," Justin said over breakfast one morning. "Just think, in 20 years we could still be eating the seeds from that same line."

"Good idea," I agreed. "That sounds delicious."

Be Calm

Bees. Makers of honey. Protectors of royalty (queens). Workers extraordinaire.

I admire bees these days, but that wasn't always the case.

My earliest childhood experiences with bees were unpleasant. My brother was stung as a little kid on a weekend visit we took to my dad's. He was allergic and his eye swelled up like a baseball. As his big sister, I felt like a failure and vowed to become more vigilant about the stinger-reared creatures.

As per usual, I took it to the extreme.

"There's a bee over there," I would announce to everyone at recess, pointing to a slide on the opposite end of the playground.

"Watch out, there are bees around here," I would mention to someone as they sat down next to a patch of clovers.

"BEE!" I would scream whenever one came near me (well into adulthood).

I knew nothing of pollination. I knew little of honey (except that you could find it in a plastic bear). I knew zilch of the dangerous decline in bee populations that had been occurring for decades.

I only knew that a couple of my Dunkerton Elementary School classmates were allergic and had to keep Epi-pens in the teacher's desk. That was enough information for me. Bees represented danger.

In recent years, I've gained new insights into the importance of bees. They play a vital role in our food system. They live in fascinating, self-sufficient communities. They make a sweet treat that can be harvested.

The first time I intentionally stood near bees was a few years ago when I spent an afternoon observing the honey extraction process at the home of a congregational member. What I know now: Beekeepers and bees have a lot to teach us the rest of us.

My husband's parents, Jerry and Nancy, have become keepers of bees. They are wrapping up their first season, and they've learned so much along the way with their first hive.

A young couple of fellow beekeepers, Noah and Lindsay, recently extracted the hive's honey for Jerry and Nancy. When Justin's parents went to pick up their honey, we were in Iowa, too, so we got to go along.

Lindsay was home at the time, and in addition to heading home with a few gallons of golden delight, we also had the chance to learn from a pro. Most fascinating to me was what she shared about uniting hives.

First of all, I had no idea that a person could unite two colonies of bees! It takes thoughtfulness and a plan (so consult an expert before you try it).

Two emotional responses by the bees get in the way of a smooth beehive uniting process: anxiety and defensiveness. If the bees of either hive become apprehensive, they will flip out and the unifying will be disrupted. If they've lost the scent of their queen, they can become particularly aggressive.

However, if the beekeeper is able to create a sense of calm for the two hives, then the bees will become one big, buzzing family.

The unifying method Lindsay prefers involves sweeping the bees from both colonies onto a large white sheet right beside the entrance of the hive. By following a series of specific steps, the bees of both hives will end up all walking in line together through the entrance.

It seems a fitting analogy for what healthy change looks in our human communities. Anxiety and defensiveness are significant impediments to unifying. But when we can nurture a sense of calm, we're all capable of connecting. We're then willing to enter into new possibilities together.

Thanks, bees, for the lesson. Calm is key.

I might not quite be ready to encourage Justin's dreams of urban beekeeping in our backyard, but I've certainly come a long way from self-elected bee safety patrol.

A change in perspective takes time, but we can savor the sweet nectar of lessons learned along the way.

The Perfect Shoes

About one Tuesday every month, I like to go thrift shopping after work. It's a special sale day at my favorite spot, and in addition to finding great deals on clothing and household goods, I find it an enjoyable activity (like going to estate sales, auctions, and garage sales).

Wandering in the footwear department one evening, I noticed a lovely, quirky pair of barely used beige shoes that would be perfect for work. "But you already have plenty of work shoes. You don't need those," I told myself.

A mild but increasingly intense sense of desire took hold. I felt I actually did need them, and I suddenly needed them very badly.

"What if someone else gets this deal instead of me? What if I never see a pair of shoes like this my size again? This footwear could change my life!" It was an urge so strong it invaded my mind, filling up all the space in my cranium.

"They're such a great deal. They're my size. I absolutely must have those shoes."

Eventually I caved and made the purchase. As I got back into my car, I paused in wonderment about whatever sensation had taken over.

Why did I feel so strongly that I needed shoes that I didn't actually need? Why did I feel so justified in procuring them as my own?

I've heard similar stories from people in regard not only to shoes, but to snow blowers, vehicles, houses, toys, dresses, antiques and books. There's a tendency inside many of us to buy and have things. We consume and we think about consuming.

It is a seemingly harmless label placed on us daily by those across all spheres of government, business and media: The American Consumer.

Pause with me for a moment and ponder. For all the immeasurable good of our current economic model, are there any dangers in referring to humans first and foremost as consumers? Aren't we more than buyers of stuff? What happens if we pause and consider the upstream and downstream implications of our purchases on the planet and the other creatures on it? In what way does being referred to as a consumer for our entire lives influence how we view ourselves?

The sensation that took over my brain at the thrift store was a kind of consumer mind. It happens to me more than is pleasant to admit. For all my self-professed desires of "tiny house living" and minimalism, I still have plenty of stuff. But it's not only about what I already have, it's also about how easy it is to imagine all the things and experiences I still want. This desire is like a water bucket with a hole in it; it never gets full.

A part of me has deeply bought into the idea that as an American consumer, I need, desire, and deserve to have *things* - especially things on sale and things that are a good deal. It's often unconscious; a quiet little push to spend and have more. But after the shoe experience, I wanted to change. I wanted to stop all thoughts of materialism. I wanted to give away everything. Change, stop, give, it would be simple. But when it comes to consumerism, I don't think the fix will be that instantaneous for me or for any of us. It's bigger than that.

According to a 2004 study by The New American Dream, many of us already recognize things are not quite right. Ninety percent expressed a belief that we're too materialistic. Ninety-one percent believed we over-consume. Ninety-three percent said Americans are too focused on work and money. Clearly, nearly all of us have noticed these consumerist tendencies in ourselves and our culture, and they've made us uncomfortable.

So now what? Perhaps the first step is simply to wake up and take notice. We can start right where we are by paying better attention to the thoughts and feelings underneath our consumption.

We can ask ourselves regularly:

How do I feel right now as I stand in line preparing to make these purchases?
Do my patterns of consumption match my spiritual values?
Are there ways I could be more intentional about how and where I consume?
Do I ever have misperceptions about what my purchases will mean for my happiness?

Awareness-building is a powerful place to begin our relationship with consumption. Our individual and collective journeys will continue with or without intentional awareness. But we'll be most equipped to manage the terrain of life if we have taken time to compassionately explore the feelings and thoughts behind the ways we consume.

Ordinary Time

The season of Ordinary Time is upon us. But ordinary can be extraordinary.

Ordinary Time is a real thing, but it's not nearly as boring as it sounds. It's one of the liturgical seasons of the church year. It's also referred to as the Season of Pentecost.

Not every congregation or denomination utilizes a liturgical calendar, and that's A-OK. There are many great ways to practice the Christian faith.

Even if your family of faith doesn't incorporate the seasons of the church year into worship, they can still be a helpful tool in your faith journey. One great quality of the liturgical calendar is the way that it connects us with brothers and sisters in faith around the world.

If your church places colored pieces of fabric (called paraments) around the altar and pulpit, it's likely they are following a liturgical calendar. Sometimes the fabric is green, red, purple, and white. Each color represents a different season.

Some of the seasons and holy days that are part of the official church year include Advent, Lent, Easter, Pentecost, Holy Trinity Sunday and Epiphany.

Ordinary Time is slightly underrated, but it's one of my favorites. Ordinary Time starts the week after Pentecost. Pentecost is the day we celebrate the Holy Spirit coming upon the early church and filling them with newfound inspiration to love and serve (see the Book of Acts, chapter 2 for more).

This year, things got officially ordinary on June 15. But Ordinary Time is not mundane. At its creation, "Ordinary Time" meant "counted time" – it was a way to mark the long stretch of weeks between Holy Trinity Sunday in June and Christ the King Sunday in November. During these months, we're often less distracted by major holidays and obligations. We have time and energy to try something new. Perhaps a new devotional practice or form of prayer. About a month ago I discovered a labyrinth on the Assisi Heights grounds. It has become a lunchtime sanctuary for me.

The Season of Pentecost provides us with a space to listen closely for the Spirit's leading. The same Spirit that led the people of the early church remains with us today.

When you look at the ordinary with patience and respect, it has a way of transforming into extraordinary right before your eyes! A blade of grass. The way your spouse makes spaghetti every Thursday. The beauty of a sunrise. The Ordinary Time of the church year serves a similar purpose. It gives us a giant span of weeks to recognize the extraordinary within the ordinary. It is not a season of glitz and glam. We aren't distracted by sales and gift lists. We get to focus on the Spirit of God at work among us. And that, dear friends, is anything but ordinary.

Church

Curators of Curiosity

Questions are important and good. It's healthy to wonder about birds and rocks and God and existence. Lean toward questions. Ask them aloud. Encourage them in others.

Our quandaries don't represent a lack of faith; they reveal courage and curiosity. Plenty of our wonderings may not have clear answers. That's fine because mysteries are lovely, too.

I am inspired by people who ask questions at church. It helps create a culture of engagement where everyone knows it's okay not to know it all. The questions can happen around worship or in Bible study or in Sunday School or during coffee hour or in the church parking lot. We can ask them to each other or the pastor or a mentor or a child. Nurturing a culture where questions are welcome is a way to create a safe space for spiritual journeyers of every age.

A couple times a month I fill in for pastors who need to be away for a Sunday. It's life-giving and energizing for me. It's also a nice way to keep a pulse on parish life now that I work at the denominational level instead of in a congregation.

One Sunday after worship while everyone was exiting the sanctuary, I stood shaking hands with folks at the door. A family of three took my breath away with their courage in asking questions.

They began by introducing themselves and then shared that they were visiting the church for the first time. After some brief conversation, they brought forth a question they had been pondering.

"We are studying the New Testament as a family, and we have some questions about Paul. Some of the things he says really bother us. We want to know more about him."

I stood amazed and then said, "I'm grateful to meet you. Yes, some of the things he says bother me, too. Let's continue this conversation."

I finished shaking hands with the rest of the line, and then our chat continued. It was a meaningful conversation in which we shared thoughts and added even more questions to the simmering stew. I expressed some of my perspectives on Paul, his letters and his historical context with the caveat that I don't have any perfect answers (side note: no one does). They asked if we could continue the conversation along the way. I said, "Absolutely." A question doesn't need to have a perfect answer in order to be worth asking.

The family then visited with other members of the church and had a chance to learn more about the congregation. A family of faith is more than a space to ask questions; it's a space to build community. Our questions are part of that. As we build relationships, serve our neighbors and spread a spirit of peace, our spiritual ponderings add flavor to the mix.

I have never thought of religious leaders as keepers of answers. Some people might believe that, but I don't. I don't think of librarians or parents or teachers or mentors as keepers of answers either. Instead, I imagine all of us to be curators of curiosity. We get to nurture spaces where people are free to wonder together. It is an honor and a privilege to do this holy work. As humans, it is work to which I believe we all are invited.

Doesn't that take some pressure off? It's okay to say, "I don't know." Even and especially within the walls of a church. Good follow-ups to "I don't know" include "Let's learn together" and "I wonder that, too."

May we all be curators of curiosity. May we receive questions gracefully. May we ask questions courageously. And may we always be willing to learn, unlearn and relearn along the way.

Living Waters

It is important for pastors to experience a sermon from a pew instead of a pulpit every now and then. I had this experience a few weeks ago in Arizona. I was near Phoenix at the time, using one of my vacation Sundays to visit a friend.

That Sunday morning at Living Waters Lutheran Church reminded me that listening to sermons can be both challenging and fruitful at the same time. I had forgotten how my mind wanders when I am not preaching or seated in the front row with the acolytes.

The sanctuary of this southwestern congregation was welcoming and spacious, with the soothing sounds of running water streaming from a fountain.

As the sermon began, I was ever-so-slightly tempted to start plotting out the remaining two days of my vacation instead of listening. Then the Holy Spirit grabbed my heart and reminded me that this was the perfect opportunity to implement some Sermon Listening Strategies. Here are my top five tips:

1) Engage. This is key! Sometimes our brains unconsciously wander just as the Bible reading ends and sermon begins. To avoid this, actively engage in what's happening. Take notes, focus, nod your head, and write down questions and thoughts for follow-up conversations with fellow parishioners or the pastor.

2) Find a nugget. Nearly every sermon ever preached has had at least one nugget worth holding onto. Many sermons have plenty. As you listen, be searching for one or two takeaways. Every single word of the sermon may not feel like it directly applies to you, and that's okay. Find a few insights and hold them tight.

3) Support the preacher. The sermon is a shared experience. Your active, listening presence is integral to the community. The way you listen and engage influences those around you. You're an important piece of the sermon puzzle.

4) Believe that God is at work. In the book of Acts, when the Christian church was beginning to spread, early leaders would preach and crowds would listen. God was at work in the midst of those sermons and worship experiences. God is still at work in the midst of sermons and worship experiences today.

It will be easier to find meaning in the sermon if you go into it believing there will be meaning to be found. If you go in a skeptic, it will most likely serve as a self-fulfilling prophecy. The Holy Spirit is present in the sermon-writing and preaching process. Believe this.

5) Offer grace. Extend a heart of compassion to the preacher and to yourself. There are a million ways to preach a good sermon and a multitude of different styles. Pastors have different strengths. Some love preaching. Some don't. Either way, the Holy Spirit works through them all.

And give yourself a good measure of grace, too. You will likely find it hard to listen sometimes. It's okay. Try again next week.

There are many meaningful parts of a worship service, and the sermon is one. God motivates, inspires, and equips us for life in this world and the next through sermons. Engage, believe and don't give up.

Book of Faith

Is the Bible true? Is it historically accurate? Are there any errors in the Bible? Does everything contained within the Word of God relate to our lives today?

Who wrote the Bible? Which parts of Scripture are about Jesus? What if I disagree with parts of the Old Testament and New Testament?

These are some of the most frequent wonderings I hear from folks after they find out I'm a pastor. Whether I'm visiting a congregation on a Sunday morning or downtown grabbing coffee on a Thursday afternoon, people are curious to know more about the Bible - and that's fantastic. They have so many great questions.

But the reality is that no one has a monopoly on the answers to any of these questions; it just depends on whom you ask. I'm far more interested in inviting people to begin a relationship with God's Word and far less interested in pretending I - or anyone else - know the eternal truths of the Universe.

Relationships take work. They require respect and understanding. Relationships have different phases; they ebb and flow. The healthiest partnerships develop over time and necessitate humility. Relationships don't generally require complete agreement between all parties; they instead benefit from a willingness to regularly express, "I hear and respect what you're saying. I care about you. And I disagree with you."

All of these relationship qualities are also true when building a connection with the Bible. Instead of solely approaching Scripture as a book of answers, what might it feel like to think of your relationship with the Bible as an ongoing, lifelong conversation?

There's an initiative called "Book of Faith" that invites people to embrace a relational, conversational approach to the Bible. You can read about it and view all kinds of handouts and resources for personal and congregational use online at www.bookoffaith.org.

Book of Faith recommends a four-fold method of reading Scripture: devotional, historical, literary and theological. It's helpful to think about these various Bible-reading methods like you'd think about the different ways to exercise. Cardio, strength training, and stretching are all good, but they each serve a unique purpose. It's useful to recognize their differences and make use of each of them accordingly.

Devotional: This is probably the most common way to read Scripture. As we read the Bible with a devotional lens, we reflect on what it means for us personally. We put ourselves into the text, and we consider how we might apply verses of Scripture to our own life situations.

Historical: The Old Testament was originally written in Hebrew, and the New Testament was first written in Greek. All of the books of the Bible came together over the course of thousands of years spanning vast changes in societal norms. When we read God's Word through a historical lens, we ask questions about the social and cultural contexts in which the words were originally written, and we also ponder the worldview and experiences of the original audience.

Literary: In addition to being a sacred tool that facilitates our connection with God, the Bible is a book. It's a big book filled with 66 smaller books. Some of these books are poetry. Some are more like newspaper stories, and still others read like a family scrapbook. When we read the Bible with a literary lens, we acknowledge it as a form of literature. We notice themes and characters. This is a way for us to honor the care that the many authors of the Bible took in crafting a compelling story that would span the ages.

Theological: Theology is defined as the study of the nature of God and religious belief. Exploring Scripture theologically is a means by which we can invite our various denominational backgrounds in as fellow conversational partners. Each denomination has its own historical texts and ways of understanding God's Word.

This reading of Scripture makes space for the multitude of contemporary theologies that exist, including process, womanist, queer, liberation, environmental and feminist. What a gift it is that we now have access to so many ways to understand God's word and to learn about how the Bible has been used to both empower and oppress.

The next time you're near a Bible, I hope you'll pick it up and take a moment to pray for God's guidance. As you turn the pages, imagine yourself interacting with a new friend. May the four-fold method of reading Scripture be a useful framework as you step forward into this new season of your relationship with the Bible.

In Some Sacred Past

Nostalgia is an interesting companion. Sometimes she shows up when I least expect it. I come to the end of a long, fulfilling day of work and crawl into bed. Suddenly all sorts of nostalgic feelings flood my mind.

Before I know it, I'm thinking back on "the good ol' days" (not that those days were that long ago). My fluffy pink prom dress. All those great times singing and playing guitar at coffee houses in college. Sitting on the porch of my Chicago apartment on sweltering summer nights.

Did all of that really happen? It went so fast. It feels like a wonderful dream.

In some ways, it is so nice to remember. It's lovely to walk through the scenes of my hazy memory. My life wasn't perfect as I lived it, but the streets in my memory are usually paved with gold and lined with smiling onlookers.

Oh, Nostalgia. At moments, you certainly get the better of me.

As much as I love the present chapter of my life, the past can sure look enticing. Sometimes I want to find a special watch that winds backward and do my life over again. I want to soak it all in one more time before I move forward.

But the hope of turning back time or living eternally in some sacred past are make-believe. In reality, time moves in only one direction:

forward.

I've noticed my friend, Nostalgia, shows up within faith communities and other organizations, too. At first, she seems so agreeable. Groups of folks sit down together, and then we share memories of how good things used to be.

It feels nice to remember. It isn't like everything was perfect 20 or 40 or 60 years ago, but in our hazy memories, we all have a way of highlighting the highs and erasing most of the lows.

Shifting Perspectives

As alluring and enjoyable as she can be, Nostalgia can also be dangerous. Sometimes we get so engrossed in the past, that we lose our ability to look forward.

Within any business, volunteer group, or religious institution, our memories of what used to be have a tendency to block our ability to see what could be.

We can approach the world in a variety of ways as we move ahead. If we let Nostalgia call the shots, then changes and fresh ideas will probably seem scary. Anything new will likely make us frustrated at how different things are now than how we remember them.

But if we invite Possibility to play a larger role in the conversation, then our perspectives might shift. We won't have to feel threatened or fearful. Instead, we can be hopeful because we know God is not bound by time or history.

God is able to weave together all possibilities from the past, present and future in order to bring love and healing to the world.

Oh, the Possibilities

There will always be nights when I will lay awake reminiscing about days gone by under my cozy comforter.

And there will always be times when all of us reflect back longingly on joyful times within our families, faith communities and other organizations. Nostalgia is a nice friend to have around once in awhile.

But Possibility is the one we want to have around every day. Possibility always invites us to look forward and have hope with every step we take.

When we look at the world around us, what will we choose to see?

Nostalgia? Possibility? Or perhaps an interesting, life-giving combination of both?

May the Holy Spirit lead us along the way and give us vision and hope for the future.

A Prairie of Negativity

Sometimes I compare myself to other people. It seems harmless at first. I notice someone's admirable trait and then immediately wish I had it.

For example, a good friend of mine is amazing at mingling with new people; he seems fully at ease in every environment. When I'm around him, I think, "I wish I was more like that! He's so cool! Why do I feel like such an awkward goofball when making small talk?"

I do this kind of comparing far too often, and it seems to happen unconsciously. I notice other people's lives and suddenly start questioning my own. I wonder: "Am I supposed to be married and have a family by now?" I find myself wishing I were prettier and had naturally highlighted hair.

Other times I compare myself to pastor friends, wishing I were a better leader or more knowledgeable about the Old Testament (why is it so hard to remember what happens in 2nd Chronicles?).

Churches sometimes compare themselves to one another, too, longing for all the things that seem great about other congregations. More young families. All kinds of volunteers. Excellent stewardship and giving.

Don't get me wrong, I believe it can be healthy to be inspired by the work of other people and churches. It becomes unhealthy when we start to disregard who we truly are in the hopes that we could be more like someone else.

At first comparing ourselves to others seems like no big deal, but it's a habit that can lead us down a treacherous pathway. It's a lot like an invasive plant.

Earlier this month, my mom and I ventured to the Minnesota Landscape Arboretum in Chaska. While there, I noticed a plaque along the trail describing three kinds of invasive plant species. I was so surprised that one of them was a kind of grass I see all the time. I had no idea!

When I saw it growing, it seemed like just another kind of lovely grass, swaying in the breeze. But it's actually aggressive and dangerous to its environment. It can take over entire areas and choke out all the other plants. Sometimes it's the flowers, trees, and grasses that seem most innocent that can do the most damage.

In the same way, each time we tell ourselves that we wish we were more like someone else, we are planting a little invasive seed in our hearts. And that seed will grow and spread, and before we know it, we will have a whole prairie of negativity growing inside.

If God wanted a world of carbon copies, that's what we would have. We would all look alike, act alike, and offer the same gifts to the world. But that wasn't God's preference. Instead, we're all different - and I truly believe God rejoices in our differences.

Celebrate exactly who God is creating you to be, and I'll attempt to do the same.

A New Chapter

It's good to stop and reflect during a time of transition. It can be an opportunity to ponder how we've grown — and imagine where God is leading us next.

Today is my last official day as associate pastor at Zion Lutheran Church in Stewartville. I mentioned in my column a couple weeks ago that I'll soon be taking a new pastoral call at the Southeastern Minnesota Synod Office in Rochester. My heart is full of gratitude for the last four and a half years. Compassionate, Gospel-centered church members. Amazing colleagues. It has been very good.

As I look back upon this life-changing chapter, so many learning moments come to mind. Here are the five most significant lessons I learned through my first call.

1) Focus on strengths rather than weaknesses. Over the last several years, I spent too much time focusing on problems. While a problem-solving approach is not bad, it tends to be draining, difficult, and not always fruitful. However, when I started investing more of my pastoral energy into building upon the congregation's multitude of strengths, a deeper joy took root.

2) Listen and encourage. I sincerely thought I needed more answers when I started out in ministry. But eventually I realized that

God wasn't especially interested in my parroted words and prayers - the things I thought I should say or do as a clergy person. Instead, the Holy Spirit was inviting me to listen and encourage. All day. Every day. These two acts — listening and encouraging — reshape people, families, and cultures. They make the dynamics of workplaces, lunchrooms, and playgrounds shift. When people feel heard and valued, they shine.

3) **Let it go.** I have to remember and re-polish this gem of wisdom every single day. People say and do weird things (myself included). Occasionally they truly mean to be hurtful, but usually they don't. In my first call as a pastor, I wasn't always the best at this and I let hurtful words and actions fester. But whenever possible, just let it go. Refocus. Don't waste precious energy and heart-space.

4) **The Holy Spirit is living, breathing, and moving.** When I started out in the parish, I didn't realize how much I'd get to witness the activity of God's spirit. It is astounding the way God is at work among all people and places. Now I'm learning to be on the lookout all the time. At funerals, weddings, lunches, Care Centers, hospitals, worship services, Sunday School, and staff meetings, the Holy Spirit is everywhere.

5) **Every voice matters; every person matters.** I have a tendency to focus the majority of my attention on people with the loudest voices. But I'm recognizing more that every voice deserves attention. Whether we are in church, at work, or around the dinner table, we benefit from drawing our attention toward those voices which are quiet and humble.

I pray that whatever transition you're facing, you, too, are able to allot some time for reflection. Each new day provides fresh perspectives. And each new chapter of life provides guidance from God that will assist us in shaping the road ahead.

Stewards of the Mysteries of God

Appliances are installed, flooring is installed, and light fixtures are installed. Museum directors install art exhibits. Computer specialists install software.

There are installations in churches, too. When a new pastor comes to a congregation, he/she is often installed. A special liturgy helps facilitate the process of welcoming a minister to her/his new context.

As part of my job, I sometimes get to be part of the installation service. It is an experience ripe with joy and gratitude for everyone involved.

The members of a church are often elated on Installation Sunday. During the special liturgy, a pastor makes commitments to the congregation, and the congregation makes commitments to the new pastor.

The minister is asked a variety of questions such as: "In the presence of this assembly will you commit yourself to this new trust and responsibility, in the confidence that it comes from God through the call of the church?"

To each question, the pastor responds, "I will, and I ask God to help me."

Then the congregation is asked a few questions, too. "And you, people of God, will you receive this messenger of Jesus Christ, sent by God to serve God's people with the Gospel of hope and salvation?"

To each question, the congregation responds: "We will."

While participating in a recent installation of a new pastor, I was struck by the beauty of the experience. Throughout the morning, I witnessed the community come together in a deeply meaningful way.

Installations need not be limited to pastors. Anyone can be installed into any position; liturgies and prayers can be created! How about installing your church council? Your Confirmation teachers and small group leaders? Your Sunday morning greeters and hospitality volunteers?

Installations aren't required to be intensely formal; the goal is only to be intentional. It's a time and space during worship to say collectively: This matters and we want to collectively ask for God's help.

There is one specific line in the liturgical order for a pastoral installation which describes an attitude I wish all humans could offer to one another. The question asked of the congregation is, "Will you regard your new pastor as a steward of the mysteries of God?"

A steward of the mysteries of God.

Stewards are people who care for what has been entrusted to them. Synonyms of the word steward include manager and administrator. A steward of the mysteries of God describes one who is responsible and thoughtful with the wonders of the Creator.

To regard one another as stewards of the mysteries of God is to respect one another in a divinely infinite sense. It is to recognize the image of God in one another. It is to honor that the mysteries of God can be named and proclaimed by all of God's children.

With this new week, take a few moments to imagine being re-installed into your role as child of God. It's an identity you've always had, but it's one we all sometimes forget.

Will you regard yourself as a steward of the mysteries of God?

Will you regard the people you encounter as stewards of the mysteries of God as well?

(If so, respond, "I will and I ask God to help me.")

Empowering Creator, equip us to step out into the world ready to show divine respect to all people - including ourselves. Form us to be faithful stewards of your mysteries. Inspire us to see your presence and your footprints everywhere. Amen.

I Will Pray for You

Imagine the scene. You arrive at work. A co-worker immediately comes over to your cubicle to tell you about some significant family updates. She's having financial and relationship struggles, and she's worried.

Now imagine another scene. You are at church. Worship is over and it's time for coffee hour. You sit down with a few of your best friends from the last several decades. One friend shares that he's been diagnosed with something serious and treatments start this week.

Versions of these scenarios happen every day all over the world. And in the midst of complicated life situations, many of us say the only words that seem to make sense: "I will pray for you."

I hear these words a lot, in and out of church. "I will pray for you" is a beautiful, meaningful way to express care and concern. It is amazing that God is available to hear us all the time. We can pray knowing that our Creator understands every word upon our lips and hearts.

One of the great challenges, however, is actually remembering to pray. This is something I continue to work on as a friend and as a pastor. I'm still learning techniques to help me follow through when I say the words, "I will pray for you." Here are a few of them:

Keep a list. I highly recommend keeping a small notepad in your purse or briefcase at all times. If you don't carry a purse, you can also keep a notecard in your wallet. Whenever a name or situation arises for which you want to remember to pray, write it down. Otherwise there are just too many things that happen in the course of the day, and it can be easy to forget. Most cell phones now have applications specifically for keeping lists, so you can keep your prayer list on your phone as well. Choose whatever format works best for you. An erasable whiteboard in the kitchen can also be a good place to keep a family prayer list that can be added to by anyone in the house.

Don't wait. If you offer to pray for somebody, sometimes it's helpful to do so immediately after the interaction. After the conversation ends, pause for a moment wherever you are (elevator, parking lot, grocery store, coffee shop), and offer up a silent prayer on his or her behalf. It doesn't have to be elaborate. Praying for someone right after you've spoken together is also a good way of transitioning back into the rest of your day. Pause. Pray. And move ahead.

Use time creatively. Sometimes it can be intimidating to even think about adding a block of time specifically for prayer. If so, consider using a block of time already built into your day. Time spent dishwashing, drying your hair, brushing your teeth, or riding the bus can all be great opportunities to spend time with your prayer list.

Stick with it. There are a lot of ways to talk to God. It takes intention but it doesn't have to be complicated - and it's never too late to start.

Faith and Doubt

I used to feel guilty about having faith-related questions. I figured that if I went to seminary, somehow all my questions about belief, the universe, Jesus and eternity would be answered. As it turned out, that was not the case.

Instead, seminary was a pathway to more questions. I met new people and experienced new viewpoints, cultures and contexts. Every class I took - like every Chicago street I followed - led me into new areas of unknowns. Looking back, I wouldn't have had it any other way.

Seminary led me to a realization that has continued to fill my veins with a steady stream of hope: faith and doubt were never meant to be enemies. Instead, they can be lifelong companions. Questions are very healthy.

My favorite member of Jesus' entourage (aka "the 12 disciples") is Thomas. Tragically, dear Thomas is regularly known as Doubting Thomas, just because he needed to see it to believe it (check out the Gospel of John, chapter 20 for the full story). Truth be told, I don't like the word doubt. It comes with so much negative baggage. I wish he could be known as Critically Thinking Thomas or Curious Thomas or Pondering Thomas. So far, none of those nicknames have stuck.

I like Thomas because he's the disciple I identify with the most. There were several occasions in the Bible when Thomas verbalized real questions about faith and following Jesus. That took guts! He could've just followed along without a thought, but that was not his style. He preferred to wonder aloud.

But not everybody is comfortable with faith-related questions. That's okay, too!

Some folks journey through life preferring to build their days on absolute certainty. Others journey through life exploring the unbeaten path and searching for cracks.

As human beings, our hearts and minds are all wired differently, and I believe one of our important life tasks is to respect other people's spiritual wiring. Besides, for most of us, the pendulum swings back and forth between having periods of questioning and periods of certainty about our beliefs.

One of my favorite parts of pastor life is weekly worship. I rejoice that every week people come together with a common understanding that we might not understand it all, but we love God, we love each other, and we're going to continue the journey.

In order to be part of a faith community, a person does not need to have all the answers. A church at its healthiest is an environment where questions are valued, God's love is assured, and all are most certainly welcome.

Peace Exchange

Interested in experiencing an extra dose of peace in your week? There was an ancient ritual created for this purpose that remains a weekly part of many worship services!

It's called The Exchange of Peace, but also goes by several other names including The Sharing of the Peace, The Passing of the Peace and The Kiss of Peace.

Right before it happens in a church service, the worship leader usually says something like, "The peace of the Lord be with you." The congregation responds in unison, "And also with you." After that, folks move about the worship space shaking hands with other people in attendance and saying something like, "The peace of Christ be with you" or "Peace" or "Peace be yours."

For those unfamiliar with the practice, it can sometimes be a surprising and uncomfortable experience. Even those who have participated in the ritual thousands of times often find it a bit awkward and confusing. We wonder how long it should last, how many people we should greet, what we're supposed to be saying and why we're even doing it in the first place.

As a way to build our collective appreciation for the exchange of peace, what follows is a brief history of the ritual and its intended purposes.

Most parts of a worship service are rooted in stories from the Bible.

This is certainly the case with the exchange of peace which has been part of worship since the very beginning of the Christian church. The sharing of a harmonious greeting is referenced in a multitude of places in Scripture.

In the gospel of John, chapter 20, verse 19, Jesus - after he rose from the dead - showed up in a locked room where the disciples were gathered. He said to them, "Peace be with you." When we share a greeting of peace during a worship service, we take our inspiration from Jesus. It's a chance to proclaim the presence and peace of Jesus to one another. It's a time to nurture our spiritual connectedness as a community and remind each other of the miraculous peace that is possible through Christ.

Another biblical story that inspired the exchange of peace comes from the gospel of Matthew, chapter 5, verses 23-24. Jesus said to his followers that if anyone wanted to make an offering to God but was experiencing interpersonal conflict, the individual first needed to seek peace and reconciliation with the other party. When we share the peace during worship these days, we're reminding ourselves and others that as Jesus followers, we are conflict resolvers and peace-seeking people.

During certain times of the year (especially cold and flu season), there are many congregations who understandably omit the sharing of the peace. Or, as an alternative, communities opt to share peace without touching.

When it comes to exchanging this sacred greeting with other people, there are many ways to do so that don't require physical contact. We can smile, nod, or bow. These options are available to you anytime if you prefer to avoid touching other people. The main goal is to compassionately acknowledge the individuals in your midst while saying, "The peace of Christ be with you."

When we share this holy greeting, we remind one another that the Spirit of God is at work in our lives and communities weaving an intricate tapestry of peace.

On the other hand, the exchange of peace is not:

• **A time to catch up with your neighbor.** The sharing of the peace isn't the appropriate time for small talk (that's better suited for before or after worship).

• **A chance to sneak out and use the bathroom.** It's helpful to consider the sharing of the peace a valuable component of a worship service and not something to be avoided.

• **An opportunity to greet everyone in attendance:** There's no pressure or historical precedent to exchanging the peace with every other person in the sanctuary. It's okay to limit your exchanges to several people and then thoughtfully return to your seat.

The peace that Jesus brings into our lives has the power to shape the way we experience the world. Sharing that peace with others during worship is a way to (1) prioritize reconciliation with one another and (2) reconnect with Jesus.

Peace

SMASH!

Planetary creation is described by NASA on its website, www.hubblesite.org, this way: "If their paths cross at just the right time and they're moving fast enough relative to each other, SMASH! - they collide, sending debris everywhere. But if they slowly meander toward one other, gravity can gently draw them together. They form a union, merging into a larger object."

This is some of the most remarkable, hopeful news I've heard in months. When bits of space matter strike each other aggressively, it creates more chaos and smaller, fragmented pieces. But when they "slowly meander toward each other," something profound takes place: the pieces unite. And then, as they gently encounter other space chunks, the planet grows.

As Americans, we are approaching another election. Inundated with combative rhetoric, divisive commercials, and an overflow of cantankerous mailings, my spirit is longing for the creation of something new in our structures of government and halls of power.

For many people of all political persuasions, the past few weeks have been exhausting. I am one such person. I am tired, hurt and confused. Sometimes I feel like a little piece of floating space material wondering what comes next.

Something new and beautiful is possible for us all and for this country, but it won't be born through chaotic, aggressive collisions of ego and antagonism. It will come about like a new planet — by taking gentle steps toward each other, walking always with warm regard and respect.

In fifth grade, my elementary school principal, Mr. Podhaski, created a new initiative centered on conflict resolution. A cohort of my classmates and I were trained as peer mediators. When a conflict would arise in the classroom or on the playground, we were trained to intervene.

We learned about how important it is to deescalate intense emotions (instead of inciting them), to give everyone time and space to share their perspectives, and to work toward a resolution to which all parties can agree.

It is mind-boggling and poignantly pathetic that we could figure it out as ten-year-olds on the playground but we cannot figure it out as adults. I believe fervently that we can do better than this.

We must stand against cruelty, bullying, and deceit. Always. It is not appropriate to intentionally create divisiveness or sow seeds of mistrust among fellow Americans. When we witness someone behaving that way, it should be a giant red flag of concern.

What new planetary possibilities await us as earthlings and Americans? How might our collective efforts build and model peace for all people?

Prioritizing conflict resolution, mutual respect and perpetual compassion may never rile up the crowds. It certainly won't be the kind of behavior that inspires internet trolls and quarrelsome commentators on cable news. But it will be the kind of rational, gentle, thoughtful behavior that makes it possible for a new chapter to begin in our country's history.

Let us proceed with care, remembering that we are all floating space dust, and trusting that together, anything is possible.

The Courage
to Disagree

Conflict can be a pathway to positive transformation. Jesus knew this. In daily interactions with the disciples and other companions, he didn't lean away from tough conversations, but leaned toward them. Honest, vulnerable disagreements are key for the development of any team, regardless of vocational context.

Last week I attended the first part of a three-part series called The Launch Project at Good Earth Village in Spring Valley. Author and leadership expert Nancy Ortberg was the speaker for the day. Ortberg is a combo platter of bold thinking, endearing humor, and authentic faith. She discussed the qualities of strong leaders.

According to Ortberg, a willingness to engage in meaningful debate and conflict is pivotal to healthy team functioning. I love this idea in theory:

- Engaging, lively conversations filled with disagreements.
- Leaders who encourage equal participation and investment by all members.
- Everyone leaving meetings feeling valued and connected.
- No backbiting or gossip or hurt feelings.

What a great vision!

In practice, I've found living into this lovely portrait of healthy team conflict to be tricky business. Words get stuck in my mouth during meetings, and disagreements sometimes give me a stomachache. I over-analyze every stinking thought before I say it out loud, and I end up leaving opportunities for conflictive collaboration wishing I had said more.

During the conference, Ortberg drew a diagram called the Thomas-Kilmann model on a large sheet of white paper. (It's interesting; Google it.) She told us that according to this model, when the members of any team (at work, church, or home) reach a point of conflict, they have five different behavioral defaults: smoothing, withdrawing, forcing, compromising, or collaborating/confronting.

Ideally, she said, we can train ourselves to confront and collaborate when conflicts arise. None of the other default options offer as much possibility for creative engagement. Good leaders bring out the collaborative nature of all team members, and meaningful collaboration generally requires an element of conflict.

Then Ortberg said something fascinating. She said Jesus is a prime example of a leader who wasn't afraid of conflict or difficult conversations: "Split a piece of paper into two sides. On one side, write down every time Jesus says something sweet or comforting. On the other side, write down every time Jesus says something conflictive or challenging. It won't take you long to realize which list is longer. Jesus knew that in order to change and transform people, conflict was required."

So I've been doing just that. I'm re-reading the Gospels and keeping a list. And she's right. Jesus does say plenty of comforting words. But the list of challenging statements is far longer. He wasn't passive-aggressive; he didn't hold back or manipulate. Jesus spoke with honesty and boldness, and he wasn't afraid of engaging his audience in lively debate. The underlying purpose of Jesus' approach: to transform lives.

In our daily environments, we, too, seek to be the hands and feet of Jesus and transform lives. Sometimes we do this through words of compassion. At other times, we do this through difficult conversations, opening our mouths when our instinct might be to stay tight-lipped. At all times, we are called to build trusting relationships and lean into conflict.

This isn't easy work. Transforming communities, churches, workplaces, and families through meaningful conflict is no small task. But perhaps confidence grows with practice. And as long as we approach it all with a spirit of love and vulnerability, there is nothing to fear.

May the transforming winds of God blow among us and equip us with the courage to sometimes disagree.

Releasing Worry

Jesus believes in our ability and willingness to redirect worry. Early on in his public ministry, he gathers a few of his first disciples together on a mountain. There, Jesus says to his new friends who had just given up everything to follow him, "Therefore I tell you, do not worry about your life."

Worry is apparently timeless. Some of the specific content of our worries has changed over time, but humans have spent large amounts of their days fixating on their problems for ages.

In our modern world, we live in a culture that actually thrives on worry and our inability to live with uncertainty. That's a lot of what worry is about: It's about what our mind does to resist the unknown. Worry is a way we try to manage uncertainty. Uncertainty, however, can't be avoided. There will always be things we don't know and can't predict.

But, when we're uncomfortable with uncertainty, our brains start to worry. Worry mimics control. It's a way to satiate that desire to prepare for what's next - even though worry doesn't relieve uncertainty in any way.

And what sorts of things do we do when we're worried? We spend money. We watch tv. We internalize and blame ourselves for everything. We eat and drink to excess. We compare our lives to other people's lives. We turn inward. We get sucked into a social media vortex.

We obsess over the news. We judge.

This is not something to feel ashamed about; it's a struggle for many of us. We're in this together. Worry was real for those first disciples who Jesus called, and worry and its implications are real for us, too.

Over the last few millennia, what do groups of people do when they're worried? What do churches do? What do countries do? We become irrationally nostalgic. We disregard the planet. We turn inward. We take advantage. We blame. We find an enemy. We fight.

Strangely, as uncomfortable as worry and our responses feel, they don't weaken the system. Instead, it only grows. We feed the beasts of consumerism and individualism. The cycle continues.

Worry sits at the center of it all.

When Jesus invites his followers to let go of worry, he's doing more than offering an inspirational quote. It's more than content for a Facebook post or an embroidered wall hanging. When Jesus says, "Do not worry about your life," he is empowering us to disrupt an entire economic and social system that feeds on our collective anxiety. Releasing worry isn't just some feel-good concept. It is revolutionary.

The reality that Jesus mentions worry to his disciples so early on is a strong signal that he recognizes just how toxic worry is to the proclamation of the gospel.

But if we're not supposed to anxiously think about the uncertainties of this earthly life, what's an alternative? Jesus says, "Strive first for the kingdom of God and his righteousness." Here, strive means to seek, to crave, and to look out for.

So what is the antidote for worry? It is being constantly on the lookout for God's kingdom. And what's God's kingdom? It is love, compassion, justice, equity, forgiveness, and peacemaking. When we spend our lives watching and working for the kingdom, Jesus says we won't need to worry.

Uncertainty is a real thing for all of us. We can't avoid it, and we don't have to try. We can, instead, learn to look at uncertainty with peace and sit alongside it. When followers of Jesus do this, imagine what's possible! It opens up so much space in our hearts and minds for the kingdom of God.

Surrounded by Noise

From the moment we wake up until the moment we go to sleep, we communicate. We transmit our ideas, thoughts and feelings in a giant assortment of ways. I encourage you to make a list of all the verbal and non-verbal ways you communicate on any given day. Give yourself some time; it will be a long list.

As central as communication is to our daily lives, it's easy to overlook its importance. When a topic is familiar, we generally assume we already know everything we need to know about it. But when it comes to effectively communicating thoughts, feelings and ideas, we all have a lot to learn! Like any other skill, good communication takes practice, and we need to keep working at it for our whole lives.

Communication impacts our personal lives, our places of work, and our communities. It also has the power to shape the way our government operates. A lot of the political volatility that continues to percolate in Washington is rooted in a lack of respect for and modeling of healthy communication. The reality is that many of us (even people in powerful positions) have never learned much about good communication, so we've done the best we can with the tools we've had available. Thankfully, we can always add more tools to the tool belt.

Step one in improving our ability to communicate effectively is to educate ourselves about how the process works. If we want to get better at sharing our thoughts and feelings, we have to understand the elements involved.

Whether we're seeking to express a thought via text, email, letter, personal conversation, or group presentation, the same general process applies. The sender of the thought chooses which communication channel she wants to use, and then she "encodes" it. The receiver then "decodes" that information.

For example, the sender wants to tell her friend about an upcoming birthday party she's hosting. She might choose to send the party information via text message. After the sender encodes the message through a text, then the recipient would have to decode the text along with any acronyms or emojis it contains. The journey from point A to point B sometimes happens seamlessly (yay!) but not always.

There are many times when communication involves distractions that can make it a challenge to encode and decode the information in the way it was intended. These distractions are called "noise."

Have you ever tried to listen to someone when you're really hungry? It's hard. That hunger is noise. Ever tried to sit through a work meeting while you're simultaneously thinking about your relative's failing health? It's almost impossible. The thoughts you're understandably having about your sick family member are also noise. Any kind of noise makes it more difficult to process information, thoughts or feelings.

We often do not know what kind of noise is going on in other people's lives, and sometimes we're not even conscious of the noise happening in our own. We can try to minimize it as best we can, but at the end of the day, it's important to give one another grace. As much as you may want your friend to get excited about your great idea, if that person is privately dealing with a major financial challenge, it will be hard for him to meaningfully process what you're trying to convey.

There is a phenomenon that surprises me daily. Two people can interpret the exact same information in totally different ways. Imagine a family who uses Facebook Messenger to communicate. If one family member expresses that they are doing "fine," some in the group chat might be concerned and interpret that word to mean that something is wrong. Others might interpret it to mean that everything is perfectly all right. But how come these different interpretations happen if it's exactly the same information being shared? It's partially due to "fields of experience."

We each have a field of experience, and all of the information that comes into our brains is filtered through it.

Your field of experience includes your life experiences, attitudes, values and beliefs. You bring it with you everywhere you go, and it influences the way you send and receive information. It was Wilbur L. Schramm who first put language to this aspect of communication back in the 1950s.

All of the people you will ever interact with have their own fields of experience. They have their own childhood histories, educational backgrounds, and personal preferences.

Please note: We have no control over other people's fields of experience. We can't control the way other people process information. We can't control another person's past or value system. All we can do is acknowledge that fields of experience are real and that they are operating all the time.

Most of the miscommunications that happen are related to noise and/or fields of experience. The more we understand these realities, the more equipped we are to manage them.

May your communications be fruitful, folks. And when we hit road-blocks, may we have the courage to address them respectfully!

Default Settings

I like my opinions. You like your opinions. Sometimes we have the same opinion, and sometimes we don't. That's natural and normal.

The default setting of a brain is to filter all incoming information in a way that supports the opinions we already have. This phenomenon is called *confirmation bias*. Every time we take in new information that supports an opinion, it feels like a special treat for our brains - like a giant piece of chocolate cake. The feeling of being right activates the pleasure center, and it feels yummy.

We basically spend our lives strengthening the beliefs, opinions, and values that we already have. This is why we're drawn to people, groups, and news outlets that support our existing worldviews. It's like eating chocolate cake all day long.

The more information we ingest, the more rooted our core values become, and core values are a big deal. They shape the way we experience reality.

Feeling fear

Shouting, statistics, angry Facebook posts and newspaper clippings are not enough to get someone to embrace another person's contrary opinion. That's just not how brains work. Brains want to feel pleasure and safety, so they're searching out information that will support their existing beliefs - not oppose them.

Presenting someone with information that counters their existing opinions doesn't activate their pleasure center - it activates their fear center, which makes people feel anxious, judged, and defensive. Instead of a delicious cake sort of feeling, it's an unsettling feeling, like being blindfolded and spun around and dropped off in an unknown location.

No wonder no one is all that quick to change their opinions, beliefs, and core values!

Most of us are happy to state and restate (and restate again) our own perspectives, but we don't like listening to opposing perspectives. And the reason is that for our brains, it feels risky, like a threat to our safety. We'd rather just eat cake and leave our brains to run perpetually in the default setting. It's a lot easier to simply listen to people who think like we already think.

Fear to freedom

There's another option, though. There's an internal software update that's free and accessible to all of us. It's not a quick download. It takes a whole lifetime and it requires regular maintenance. It's worth it, though. It's a path that leads from fear to freedom.

Buried inside all of us is the option to shift from auto-pilot into manual. If we make this change, we can take in information in ways that free us to form alternative opinions, develop different core values, and expand our worldviews.

It's important to note that making the most of the manual brain setting requires a willingness to be wrong. This is no small task. In fact, it's one of the most difficult tasks of all. But it gets easier the more we practice.

The trick is to help our brains remember that being wrong is okay and safe. We won't internally combust if we trade in our old opinion for a new one. Brains like to be right because they like to feel safe. We can be wrong and still be safe. When we understand this, the fear center of our brains calms down.

We're then able to hear about someone else's worldview without becoming enraged and defensive.

When we remind ourselves of this important reality, we begin to become more comfortable hearing viewpoints entirely different from our own. It's humbling in a beautifully powerful way. We become more open and less fearful, and that frees up all kinds of space in our hearts and minds.

We can understand

It's tempting to believe that the people of this country are so divided that we'll never be able to understand one another. But that's a lie; a total, complete lie. And a lot of executives are making a lot of money off of us believing that myth and being sucked into a media vortex 24 hours a day.

Why are we so sucked in? For a very understandable reason: because watching and reading media that supports the beliefs we already have is like consuming chocolate cake non-stop. While it might feel good to the pleasure centers of our brains, it's still giving us indigestion. We are a country with a massive case of gut rot, and it's time to add some vitamins and minerals back into the diet.

We all have a lot to learn from each other, and we're not going to learn it by watching and listening to opinions exactly like the ones we already have. So let's turn off the noise and get to work. We've got a lot of listening and learning to do.

A Global Reset

Reality is heavy. Last weekend we saw images of hundreds of white supremacists gathered for a rally in Virginia. We heard the horrifying news that one of them drove a car into a crowd of people killing one and injuring nineteen. A few days before that, we witnessed two world leaders threatening one another's people with nuclear warfare. We saw government leaders in Guam creating preparedness documents to equip residents in case of a missile strike. We imagined what life is like right now for children in Virginia, North Korea, South Korea and Guam.

It doesn't seem real. How can this be? What are the roots of violence and how can we get rid of them? How can we free ourselves and our neighbors from the toxic grip of fear?

I am drawn to the words Jesus once said to an exhausted crowd: "Come to me all who are weary and carrying heavy burdens, and I will give you rest" (Matthew 11:28). I imagine the whole world sitting in a giant circle holding hands then laying down for a nap. I wish all seven billion of us could enjoy a collective snooze. We could set our alarms and then wake up at the same time. It would be a global reset. We'd awaken refreshed and aware.

I long for a day without slander and defensiveness. For a country less divided. For a world where everyone gets to go to school and drink clean water. For a population eager to embrace humility and forgiveness. For people ready to admit mistakes and acknowledge privilege and inequity.

Jesus understood exhaustion. He lived in a chaotic time, too. He often wandered off to hillsides to pray. He regularly gathered his friends with him to eat. He probably worked in his woodshed when he wasn't on the road. When he was weary, he sought rest.

We are weary, and we need rest, too. The resting part matters. Turning off the news now and then matters. Meditating and praying and sleeping matters. If you're exhausted from all this hurt and you're infuriated by those stoking the fires, then take a nap from all of it for awhile. Power down your phone. Turn off your cable and Internet. Get the television out of your bedroom. Turn on classical music. Go to the library. Teach your dog a new trick. Rest.

Resting is what restores us to reenter the world ready to serve. We need you. So rest up.

But remember: Jesus didn't call his followers to retreat entirely and permanently from the world's wounds. Instead, he encouraged them to acknowledge hurt and sickness. He didn't say, "Oh, injustice is too painful for you? Okay, no problem, go back to your iPhone." He said, "With the help of the Holy Spirit, you can handle this."

Like Mordecai said to Esther when it was time to stand up to oppression, "And who knows but that you have come to your royal position for such a time as this" (the Old Testament book Esther tells the full story).

We're not royalty, but we do have power. We do have a sphere of influence. Our voices matter. And now is a really important time. Peace is not partisan. Compassion is not partisan.

Jesus perpetually invites his followers to get out and do something about injustice, pain and suffering. He once told the story of a man who risked his safety and his health to help a person who was hurting (Luke 10:25-27). Even when no one else was willing to show mercy, this man was. Jesus advised his listeners, "Go and do likewise."

His timeless guidance remains. Go and do likewise. We rest. We recharge. And we serve. It's a cycle. There is no beginning and no ending. This is the life to which we are called.

In 1955, Jill Jackson-Miller and Sy Miller collaborated on the song, "Let There Be Peace on Earth." The stanzas make a fitting daily prayer for all of us.

> *Let there be peace on earth*
> *And let it begin with me;*
> *Let there be peace on earth,*
> *The peace that was meant to be.*
> *Let peace begin with me,*
> *Let this be the moment now;*
> *With every step I take,*
> *Let this be my solemn vow.*
> *To take each moment and live each moment*
> *In peace eternally.*
> *Let there be peace on earth*
> *And let it begin with me.*
> *Amen.*

The Peace and
Unity of Christ

Congregations are communities. At their healthiest, they are safe places for asking questions, proclaiming forgiveness, and experiencing the full range of human emotions. Congregations are made up of regular human beings spurring one another toward peaceful, authentic, justice-oriented lives.

Generally, churches have leaders, and these leaders are often called pastors. In the branch of the Lutheran church of which I am a part, when a congregation welcomes a new pastor into their midst, there is a special order of service called an "installation." Perhaps your family of faith participates in something similar.

Part of my job now is to occasionally go out to congregations around southeastern Minnesota and facilitate these installations. Last Sunday I got to install a pastor at both of the congregations she now serves, and it was a breathtakingly life-giving experience.

The installation provides opportunities for both the pastor and the church members to make commitments. The pastor commits to being responsible, faithful, and confident in such a way that "God's love may be known" in all he/she does. The pastor responds to each question, "I will, and I ask God to help me." The words of the response are a reminder that pastors don't live on islands of their own inspiration. They are tethered always to God, and depend on God's help.

After the pastor makes his/her commitments, the congregation is invited to do the same. The people of the church commit to "pray for her/him, help and honor her/him for her/his work's sake, and in all things live together in the peace and unity of Christ." The congregation responds with the words: "We will, and we ask God to help us."

Easy words to say. Challenging, profound words to live out: "To live together in the peace and unity of Christ." Peace AND unity. Imagine it. Imagine what that would look like just in your own family of faith. Now imagine every congregation in your area living in peace and unity.

Now imagine it spreading to your whole state, country and throughout the world. All of us vowing to live together in the peace and unity of Christ. That's the kind of intention that changes things - a collective vision of peace. It starts small, in our own individual hearts, and it spreads: to families, congregations, denominations, countries, and beyond.

There is no point during an installation when everyone vows to agree on everything. To live together in the peace and unity of Christ is not to ignore our feelings or avoid dissension. It's normal and healthy to have differences of opinion in our congregations and elsewhere. The goal isn't to always agree.

Instead, the goal is to enter into any differences rooted in a shared valuing of peace and unity in spite of all that might separate us. It's possible to disagree in peace. It's possible to have conflict and still be unified. It's not easy work, but we are called to do it.

In the week ahead, let's commit to living together in the peace and unity of Christ. With our families, friends, and co-workers. With our exes, in-laws, and political foes. In all of our interactions, let's do what we can to live together in peace and unity because that's the starting point of global change. The starting point is within our own hearts and within our own spheres of influence.

We will do this important work together, and we ask God for help.

We Lost our Words

Here we stand on the precipice of Election Day. We've almost reached the summit of a rigorous climb, and the view from here remains hazy.

Together, we hope and pray that when the endless fog of political noise and commentary fades, we'll be left looking out on a landscape that leaves us hopeful and encouraged.

Tuesday and the days following will be full of emotion. For some, there will be great joy. For others, deep frustration. There will be new representatives, senators, and judges - and we will also elect a new president.

While all of those elected officials prepare to take on their new roles, we will be preparing for a different assignment. We will be getting reacquainted with our lifelong mutual obligation: loving each other (see John 13:34).

Like partners who've gone a long while without even a touch, we, too, have lost our way from each other. We've forgotten that regardless of party affiliation, we're all on the same team. This election season got ugly and gross, and many of us grew so angry we lost our words. We blamed. We judged. We got swept up in the tornado of mass-produced digital sensationalism.

On Wednesday, Nov. 9, the page will turn. One chapter will end and another will begin. We will wake up and continue to live our lives.

We will do what we do. Stir coffee. Buckle seat belts. Chew cereal. Swallow meds. Read books. Deliver casseroles. Rake leaves.

In a few days, all the political signs will come down. With that unobstructed view, it will be easier to remember all the things we have in common. We will be reminded that regardless of how we voted and regardless of the election results, we'll keep sharing the land with which we have been entrusted.

Zen teacher Thich Nhat Hanh writes in his book <u>How to Love</u> about five awarenesses that can be practiced by "anyone at anytime to help safeguard our relationships." The 'fifth awareness seems particularly fitting and timely for our country. The author writes, "We are aware that blaming and arguing can never help us and only create a wider gap between us; that only understanding, trust, and love can help us change and grow."

I don't want a wider gap than the one which already exists. With Thich Nhat Hanh's awareness in mind, I offer a blessing for today and the days ahead.

When the newsmakers tempt us with titillating headlines,
And we see no sign of respectful discourse,
May we have courage to turn off the noise
And tune back into our real lives.
When we step into our yards,
And remove the signs we planted with hope,
May we choose optimism and mutual respect.
When the leaders we elected step into their new roles,
And the true work begins,
May they speak and act with humility, respect, and courage.
When all the ballots have been cast,
And we have again celebrated the gift of democracy,
May our hearts turn wholly toward love.

Justice

The Entitlement Hulk

On a recent Tuesday afternoon, I was heading home from work during the epic Rochester rush hour. At the intersection of Elton Hills Drive and Assisi Drive, I found myself at the end of a long line of cars. We were all waiting for the left arrow to turn green.

When it finally happened, something in me turned green, too - like The Hulk. As the long line of cars crept slowly forward, I became irritated. "Come on! Hurry up!" I thought. "That green light is mine!"

I was consumed by the flame of entitlement. I felt I deserved that one specific green arrow. And so, as the arrow switched heartily into the yellow end of the color spectrum, I snuck through at the last possible legal second. The Entitlement Hulk relaxed, and I morphed back into something closer to human.

Entitlement is defined as, "the belief that one is inherently deserving of privileges or special treatment." Entitlement is nothing new; people have felt deserving of special privileges since the beginning of time. It is a consistent theme in the Old Testament, the New Testament, and basically every chapter of every World History book. That being said, there are some unique aspects of the type of entitlement taking root in our particular cultural context, and the consequences are alarming.

Paul Piff is a social psychologist in California, and his research has revealed that the more people have, the more they think they deserve. His studies have shown that an increased sense of entitlement can lead an individual to become increasingly mean and more likely to cheat and exploit others. Yikes! The ramifications of all this play out daily on a local and global level. The attitude of entitlement is tangled into the root system of many systemic injustices.

Thankfully, there is another way, and it begins with our own lives and choices. Flipping through the pages of the Gospels, it's clear Jesus knew about the Entitlement Hulk that lives inside us all. So to counter it, he says things like "Whoever wants to be first should be last." He speaks in ways that invite us to reorient our compasses away from a perpetual focus on self so that we might stop squishing each other.

At the core of a sense of entitlement is a feeling of being superior to other people. That perspective is like quicksand. It's easy to get sucked in, and it's hard to get out. But it's a lie. We can choose a different viewpoint.

Releasing our entitlement tentacles doesn't mean withdrawing to a life of complete self-sacrifice leading to our own detriment. We're looking for a middle ground. What might it look like to value ourselves deeply and value everyone else deeply, too? Could it be possible to build a world where our collective sense of empathy is far stronger than our collective sense of entitlement?

I'd like to give you a little homework assignment. In the days ahead, complete this sentence: "Everyone on the planet should have _____."

There's no universally accepted right answer here. This is meant to be food for thought. So make a list. Talk about it with your family, friends or Bible Study group. Ask your kids for their opinions. What are the things everyone deserves? And if the world is too big a canvas, start with your own community. To what is everyone in this community entitled? Food? Clean water? A safe place to sleep?

Whatever appears on your list, I encourage you to think about how we will all work together to create that sort of world. It will require compassion. It will require hard work and fierce determination. It will require a world full of people willing to say: my life isn't only about me; it's about us all.

News Fatigue

When it comes to global awareness, what are my responsibilities as an inhabitant of this planet? I'm struggling to discern the most appropriate answer to this quandary. What am I called to care about and pray about? What are the best uses of my energies and resources?

Lately, I'm overwhelmed by all media. I have a case of news fatigue. There's just so much happening all the time. And the events aren't insignificant. Destructive earthquakes, communities in strife, outbreaks of disease. Airstrikes and warfare. Hunger and poverty. It's all real, it all matters, and it's all happening every day.

At book group last week, we sat together on lawn chairs with books on our laps and snacks in our hands. The fireflies danced around the yard, and we pondered life's mysteries together. Like, "How is it that on the same planet such terrible things and beautiful things can be happening at the very same moment?"

It's easier to pay attention to the lovely parts of life. They make us feel joy and gratitude. It's healthy to take moments to appreciate beauty. But the terrible happenings in our world deserve attention, too. Otherwise, how will we learn how to work together to make existence less awful for those being impacted?

I feel guilty when I don't take time to read the paper or watch the news or listen to public radio. I feel overwhelmed when I do take time to absorb a bit of what's happening. Where is the middle ground?

When it comes to finding this holy ground, I don't know exactly what to do or where to start, but I have faith that, together, we can figure this out. Likely, you already have some excellent strategies up your sleeve for remaining globally conscious without turning into a knot of worry, fear, and hopelessness.

Not paying any attention to the events of the world doesn't feel like the right option. I want to be aware but I don't want to get swallowed up. This is the plan: I'm going to set a timer and read the paper for 15 minutes every day. I know it's not much, but it's something. And while I read the paper, I'm going to make a prayer list. Then I'll spend five minutes praying about all that I've read, expressing gratitude for the joyful stories and petitions for the world's brokenness.

Maybe by combining awareness with immediate prayer, a sense of hopefulness can pervade. If you'd like to join me in this endeavor, please adapt it in whatever ways make the most sense for you.

I wonder how the Spirit might move among us if we all devoted five sincere minutes a day to praying about what is happening across our community, country, and world. What if we turned off the TV when the news was over and prayed about what we saw? What if we turned off the radio for the last five minutes of the drive and prayed about what we heard? The prayers don't need to be complicated. I imagine that any one of author Anne Lamott's three favorite one-word prayers would apply nicely: "Help," "Thanks," or "Wow."

Sometimes the complexities of global issues can seem insurmountable. But nothing is impossible with God. Jesus says as much: "Everything is possible for those who believe" (Mark 9:23). That idea works as a useful prayer, too: "God, break into this seemingly hopeless situation with your infinite possibilities."

At the end of the Gospel of Matthew, Jesus says, "And remember, I am with you always, to the end of the age" (Matthew 28:20). Jesus doesn't disappear. He promises to be with us forever as the eternal guiding force in our lives. This is an important reminder when we feel fatigued and exhausted by all the fragmented pieces of our planet. Jesus is with us, and His beacon of light can always guide our hearts toward hope.

God of peace, we have access to so much news and information. HELP us to use these tools in the shaping of a just world. THANKS for providing ways for us to be connected. WOW, we are inspired by a sense of connectedness to all your people.

Spirit, no matter what the headlines read from day to day, remind us that you are near and everything is possible.

Great America

"How did we get in this mess?" a friend wrote in a recent email about the presidential election.

My initial thought: "I have no idea, but the whole thing is making me want to upchuck on a daily basis."

Then I considered the question more deeply. As it turns out, I have an idea about how we got into this mess: a national history of widespread racism, misogyny and discrimination.

Our country was founded on a lot of beautiful aspirations by some exquisitely brave individuals. When the Declaration of Independence was signed on July 4, 1776, what a joy it must have been to imagine living in a country rooted in the belief "that all men are created equal, that they are endowed by their Creator with certain unalienable rights, that among these are life, liberty and the pursuit of happiness."

It must have been especially awesome if you happened to be a white man on July 4, 1776. But, for the rest of society, it was probably not quite as cool.

From the start of this country, the system was rigged against people who were born anything other than white and male. And even for those born white and male, there were a lot of economic inequities that made the system unjust for them, too.

Great America

This country is great; I am incredibly thankful to live here. But it was also built upon a lot of evil. Early Americans stole land from native peoples. Huge injustices remain in the treatment of Native Americans today.

Slavery was legal until the 13th amendment was ratified on Dec. 6, 1865. Segregation was legal until the Civil Rights Act of 1964. Massive racial inequities remain embedded throughout the workplaces, colleges, schools, prisons, and households of our country. Women didn't get to vote until 1920.

To this day, the gender wage gap is at least 20 percent, with a much larger gap in some industries. The LGBTQ community finally gained marriage rights last year, but people of orientations other than heterosexual continue to face ongoing discrimination.

Have we made progress? Yes! Absolutely! And that progress is definitely worth celebrating. But, if, indeed, we're all created equal, we still have a way to go in living into that aspiration.

This is all part of our national history. Alongside huge advances in technology, economics, education, global relations and many other beautiful happenings, we also have a history of racism, misogyny and discrimination.

Closet cleaning

So, to answer my friend's question, how did we get into this mess? Well, perhaps over the years, we stuffed the national family closet with a whole lot of secrets. Now the closet is full. It's spilling out, and all our skeletons are now in front of us. We are coming face to face with what happens when generations of human beings do not recognize the worth and personhood of other human beings.

It's shocking to see all the misdirected violence, verbal aggression, bigotry, and religious intolerance around us. It's overwhelming. So we understandably try and shove it all under the bed. We deny it exists. We chalk it up to "locker-room talk" and distract ourselves with football and the newest celebrity couple news.

What else do we do with all those incendiary skeletons? Well, perhaps we unknowingly catapult those bigoted bones right onto center stage disguised as a political candidate.

Say what you want about our presidential nominees, but those candidates are part of us. Both of them. They are in the positions that they are in because we empowered them to be there. So if we are disgusted, then maybe we need to set a new collective standard around acceptable behavior. Maybe we need a different set of boundaries around permissible and impermissible conduct, and when those boundaries are violated, there need to be consequences.

As the people of this country, it is within our rights to reclaim the power that we have. We can set a healthier, saner standard for communication than what we've been witnessing lately.

Big steps

The healing of the nation will come through our shared commitment to standing up to oppression in all forms. It will take a lot of courage, empathy, listening, and self-reflection. It will require vulnerability and responsibility. Our greatest healing will come when we're willing to bravely admit that we're walking through a graveyard of centuries-long systematic oppression in this country. And after we admit them, we will need to commit to address them one by one.

Right now, we are faced with questions as a country: Who are we? Who will we be? How will we treat each other? How will we talk about our genitals and the genitals of others? What will we teach our children about respect, love, and power?

We are provided opportunities to strive for renewal, hope, and change even (especially) in the midst of challenging times. As we shape the next chapter of our national future together, let's pause to consider the past and work our way through those skeletons. So much possibility and hope can come out of facing our brokenness and fears.

I know the political climate can feel frustrating and exhausting right now, but don't give up or check out. It's certainly messy. But the great thing about a mess is that it's only temporary. Together, we have a chance to clean it up.

Pipestone

Help us to remember the sacredness of this place of peace, guide us, open our hearts and minds so that we might see the beauty in each other and all things that are of your creation.

These words are a portion of a beautiful prayer etched into cement just down the road from Pipestone National Monument. My mom, Pam, and I explored the site over the weekend. We walked away feeling awe and inspiration. Being the Iowa girls that we are, we also left the park feeling compelled to learn more about Minnesota history.

I wasn't especially interested in local or world history growing up. I learned what I needed to learn to get good grades, but the facts and stories didn't make a permanent indentation in my heart or mind. I am embarrassed to admit it, but for a long time, I found history boring and irrelevant.

It was a naive perspective, since I now understand that history is just about as interesting and relevant as it gets. But what can I say? I'm a work in progress. Adulthood has revealed that an awareness of the past is immensely helpful in understanding the present and envisioning the future. History is a profound teacher. But, like any classroom setting, student engagement is critical; the teacher is only one part of the equation.

So now I'm trying to make up for lost time by filling in all my knowledge gaps, and let me tell you - there are significant gaps. As I learn and relearn as an adult, this time I want it all to stick! I wish I could find a giant Costco-size jar of brain glue, and use it to paste facts, maps, and stories permanently into my temporal lobe.

There are so many parts of Pipestone National Monument I want to remember. Especially impactful were the bits of history we learned about various tribes of American Indians. We watched a 22-minute video in the visitor center that outlined the geologic and cultural history of the region and the religious importance of pipes and pipestone. Historically, many different tribes came to the quarry to harvest the red pipestone rock to make their pipes. Pipestone carving is a special art and is still practiced today.

I'd like to glue into my mind...

+ The beauty of walking around the quarry at sunrise.
+ The deer that bounded across the prairie as we stepped onto the trail.
+ The Oracle and Old Stone Face, rock formations with immense spiritual significance.
+ The sensation of being suddenly and overwhelmingly compelled to hug a huge oak tree near a waterfall.
+ The injustices perpetrated against many tribes of American Indians in Minnesota over the years and the resilience and courage they have exhibited in spite of such cruelties.

I want to remember it all.

There is a legend that the Great Spirit told all those who entered the land around the present-day Pipestone National Monument that it was a sacred place and no weapons could be used or brought upon it. Abiding by this guidance, it is widely believed that even warring tribes would put down their weapons and quarry together for pipestone in peace.

One of history's greatest strengths is that it reveals what's possible. Peace is possible - even among enemies. The more we understand both the triumphs and the mistakes of the past, the more equipped we will be to build a peaceful, just future for all creation.

A morning in Pipestone renewed within me a desire to keep learning about the history of this state and its inhabitants. The opening words of the prayer imprinted just down the road from the park's entrance remain within me as an ongoing refrain.

Help us to remember.

A Song of Joy
in Your Heart

Western South Dakota is a place of wonder. My mom, Pam, and I traveled there earlier this fall. We explored Wall, Rapid City, Deadwood, Hill City, Keystone, and the Badlands.

There were many moments on the adventure when I had no words to describe the beauty. I could only breathe in and out - in total awe that such a place exists (and only about nine hours away). It is a deeply spiritual place, and the holiness literally twinkles off the Sioux quartzite.

In Deadwood, we visited the museum Tatanka: Story of the Bison. It is a building on a hill just outside of town that weaves together the story of the Lakota people and the *tatanka* (Lakota for bison). Photos and essays describe how the early white settlers slaughtered the bison to near extinction from the 1830s to 1860s. It is an awful tale of irrevocable gluttony.

Billy, an employee at the museum and a member of the Lakota nation, gave an informal presentation. He spoke with a poignant openness and graciously welcomed any and all questions with the caveat, "Ask me anything. I'm not easily offended."

As Billy shared about the history of the Lakota in South Dakota, my heart grew increasingly heavy. It is a heaviness that persists. There are many wonderful things about this country, and I am very thankful to be a citizen. But there are chapters of our history that are terrible, and we can't undo them through avoidance. The healing of these national wounds comes only through the acknowledgement of them - and a willingness to learn not only from the triumphs of our ancestors but also their trespasses.

The violent removal of American Indians from their lands, homes, and traditions is a tragedy that was brought to the forefront of my mind while in South Dakota. That period in history is a clear example of what happens when an unquenchable thirst for more surpasses a people's collective ability to recognize the consequences of their actions.

At the museum, I learned that the Lakota used every possible bit of the bison they hunted. The bladder became a water vessel. The horns became bowls and spoons. The fur became blankets and clothing. When I asked Billy about the core spiritual teachings of the Lakota, he uplifted the importance of mutual respect and the centrality of community. He also expressed the key teaching to never take more than is needed. Such timeless, powerful guidance.

Mom and I walked around the outdoor statue garden after looking at the indoor exhibits. Outside we saw the bronzed buffalo creations of artist Peggy Detmers portraying a traditional Lakota bison hunt. As we walked around the sculptures, instrumental music played over the outdoor speakers. The musician spoke at the end of the song: "Carry a song of joy in your heart. And may we all be one."

Those words reflected the spiritual guidance my heart longed for in that moment: a song of joy and a prayer for the unity of all things.

The web of all creation - past, present, and future - seemed so apparent in western South Dakota. Upon arrival back in Minnesota, I realized the same is true here. Everything is connected: the rocks under our feet, waterways, trees, fossilized bones in the ground, historical documents, politics, aspirations of generations past, and present-day hopes for tomorrow.

In a world so profoundly connected, the musician's prayer rings eternally true: May we all be one.

Build this World
from Love

Religious buildings like churches, synagogues, temples and mosques are sometimes referred to as "houses of God." In both the Old Testament and the New Testament of the Bible, there are a multitude of occasions in which the Creator interacts with human beings; the physical space of the interaction is then referred to as God's house.

On Saturday, Oct. 27, 2018, an act of violent anti-Semitism took place at a house of God. It was during a service at the Tree of Life Synagogue in Pittsburgh that eleven people were killed and seven were injured.

In the week after the shooting, the B'nai Israel Synagogue in Rochester hosted a Gathering of Reflection and Response. All community members were invited to attend. As I looked around the synagogue during the gathering, surrounded by an immense crowd of peace-loving people from a multitude of faith traditions, I had a permeating sense of sitting inside God's house. Prayers of healing, grief and peace were offered. Children and adults read passages from holy texts. Poems were recited. Songs were sung. God's spirit was woven like a thread through the whole service.

At the beginning of the evening, Rabbi Michelle Werner, the leader of the community, encouraged us to be explicit in our naming of the shooting as anti-Semitic. She reminded us that what happened was more than a tragedy. It was an act of anti-Semitism directed at Jewish people. The definition of anti-Semitic is, "hostility toward or discrimination against Jews as a religious, ethnic, or racial group."

In naming the root of the violence for what it was, we as a society can face it more honestly and address the underlying causes more directly.

In these days since the service at B'nai Israel Synagogue, I've been thinking a lot about anti-Semitism. Growing up in a very small town in Iowa, I never knew a Jewish person or had much exposure to Jewish traditions. It wasn't until I attended seminary in Chicago that I started to learn more about Jewish history and customs. It was during those years that I began to comprehend the ways that the New Testament of the Bible and Jesus' teachings have been used in anti-Semitic ways to oppress and discriminate against Jewish people for many hundreds of years.

Discrimination, threats and violence continue to be part of the lived experience of Jewish people in our country and around the world. For those of us who identify as Christian, it is very important that we keep alert to the ways our religious texts, history, practices and customs have been harmful to Jewish people. Not only must we pay attention to these injustices, we must repent and do what we can to chart a different path.

I give profound thanks to Rabbi Werner and the members of B'nai Israel Synagogue for creating a holy space of community and connectedness during the Gathering of Reflection and Response. It was a gift to be together and to sense God's nearness with us.

One of the songs that we sang during the service was called, "Olam Chesded Yibaneh." The lyrics were an encouragement to build always from a foundation of love. May they be our collective prayer and our ongoing hope:

Olam chesded yibaneh
I will build this world from love
And you must build this world from love
And if we build this world from love
Then God will build this world from love.

Use Your Power

It's an important time to be a man in the United States. I identify as female, and I don't know what it feels like to be a man right now. However, I can imagine that lately it feels a bit unsettling and uncertain. It's a confusing time.

It's a pivotal moment for women, people of color, immigrants, and the LGBTQ community, too, but for this column, I'd like to address men, and specifically white, heterosexual, Christian men who were born and raised in this country.

First off, you matter. Your experiences matter. Your voice matters. You have valuable ideas and perspectives. You work hard. I'm not here to blame or shame you for being a white, heterosexual, Christian man. I'm glad you're you; there's no one else who will ever experience reality quite like you. You're important.

In this season of Advent, a time of preparation, I invite you to journey with me deeper into a conversation about power. This is one way we can prepare ourselves for the new story God is writing in our midst.

Have you ever played Monopoly? Everybody starts out with the same amount of cash. But what if some players were to start with extra? It's possible they wouldn't even notice it at first. Maybe they'd have no clue they even had the advantage. But whether they ever realized it or not, the whole game would be rigged and unfair. The distribution of power wouldn't be equal.

In this life and in this country, we don't start out with the same amount of power, and the system is rigged from the beginning. To fix the rigged game, everyone has to be willing to ask hard questions and look objectively at the system as a whole.

For those of us who are white, we have extra power from the moment we are born simply because we're white. It's not fair and it's not right, but it's real. For those who are white and male, you have even more inherent power right from the start. If it were that rigged game of Monopoly, it's like you started the game with a stash of houses, extra $500 bills, and a couple get-out-of-jail-free cards.

For many, this interpretation of reality is a difficult pill to swallow, but please keep walking with me. I believe in your capacity to look at this topic without getting defensive.

Perhaps you have experienced significant tragedy in your life. Maybe you are or have been very poor. It's possible you feel that you have no power. Perhaps you've worked extremely hard your whole life, and you feel you've earned every dime. I hear your frustrations. It's true; not every white man starts out with the same amount of power, and many of you have experienced very real oppression and disadvantages along the way.

But rather than getting stuck in this spot on the trail, shutting down, and dismissing what I'm saying, please just hold my hand and keep walking. You didn't create this rigged game, and it's not your fault. But you can help fix it, and you can boldly support those who have been harmed by it.

As white males, you don't have to be ashamed that you have power. You can use your powerful, important voice for good; you can dismantle the injustices one small step at a time. Power isn't something to be ashamed of; it's something to share and to use as wisely as possible.

There are different ways to respond to the recent uptick in news coverage of sexual harassment, sexual assault, and people in positions of power losing their jobs because of poor decisions.

In conversations I've had with men over the past few weeks, I've noticed a few patterns of response: 1) dismiss it and laugh it off; 2) blame and discredit women; or 3) take an honest look within and admit that the system is broken.

I invite you to consider the third style of response. When you hear your friends and peers defaulting into the first two kinds of responses, I encourage you to use your power to intervene.

I was at lunch with two men last week and one of them said, "As I have been watching the news this week, I've realized that I have been that guy. I've been the one making those inappropriate jokes. I've been the harasser, and I'm embarrassed by that."

I said, "That's a brave and self-aware thing to admit. Thank you for having that kind of courage. Thank you for being willing to change and to help fix the system."

At several points in the Gospels, Jesus invites his followers to "Take courage!" Now is the time for courage. We all need giant, daily injections of courage. Together we journey onward ready to dismantle all that is unjust, ready to be part of the solution, and ready to share power in ways that affirm the value of every person.

Shamar the Earth

God believes in the deep and exceeding goodness of creation and invites us to do the same. One way we can honor the profound splendor of the cosmos is by advocating for it in intentional ways.

A special report was released earlier this month by the Intergovernmental Panel on Climate Change (IPCC). The report outlined the serious consequences of climate change that are already being experienced. As described in the frequently asked questions guide that accompanied the document, "Climate change represents an urgent and potentially irreversible threat to human societies and the planet."

The IPCC's report makes clear that all people in all countries need to act immediately to limit the increase to 2.7 degrees Fahrenheit (1.5 degrees Celsius).

As I was trying to wrap my mind around the report and its accompanying documents, I read a short allegorical story about climate change by Kate Marvel. It's well worth a read: blogs.scientificamerican.com/hot-planet/slaying-the-climate-dragon.

The story is set in a magical kingdom and climate change is portrayed as dragons who become harder and harder to ignore. Marvel's story is a helpful conversation partner to add to the mix as we seek to understand the severity of the changing climate.

As people of faith, what are our responsibilities during all this? How are faith and climate related? How is the Spirit calling us to respond to the cries of the planet? What resources, tools and skills do we need to follow Jesus into this changing world and climate?

These are questions not just for climate scientists but for us all. Avoidance of the topic and ignorance will get us nowhere. Ninety-one authors and review editors from 40 countries came together to create the IPCC report, and it was based on 6,000 scientific references. The climate is changing. It matters. There is still time to respond.

Following Jesus means we can courageously face the truth and keep going even when it's hard.

We are at an important moment in which it will be imperative for people of faith to reaffirm our collective commitment to advocating for a more compassionate regard for the planet we inhabit. The Old Testament book of Genesis provides a framework to empower us to understand the gifts and responsibilities that come with being a human on Earth.

In Genesis, we encounter two powerful creation stories; each provides layers of depth and beauty. These are not scientific depictions of exactly what processes took place when the universe began. Instead, these chapters of God's Word are true poetic gifts meant to enhance our understanding of the creativity and compassion of a God who chose to make creation possible. Wondrous!

The first creation story is described in Genesis, chapter one. On each of the first six days, God adds something new to creation, and on each day, the Creator proclaims its goodness. On the sixth day, God says it's not just good but very good. Genesis was first written in Hebrew; the Hebrew word for "very" is *mehode*. It means exceedingly, abundantly, and completely. Reading Genesis chapter one is an invitation to experience deep awe and gratitude for the universe and our planet.

In Genesis 2:4, we encounter a second creation story. This one is magnificent, too. It's here that we are invited to ponder the role of humans in the midst of creation. In Genesis 2:16, after God creates Adam and Eve, God surrounds them with a lush garden to "till and keep it." The Hebrew word for "keep" is *shamar*. *Shamar* is a word with many layers of meaning. Its synonyms include observe, guard, preserve, and regard.

When I hear about the seriousness of climate change, I am reminded of a God who trusts in our capacity to guard and preserve our planet. As humans, we are entrusted with the responsibility of *shamar*-ing the world around us.

The response that is required is multifaceted. It will require the collaboration of individuals, communities and countries. The private and public sector will both play a role in healing our earth. Our household choices will certainly continue to matter, but the responsibility of governments and businesses to change the tides of climate change cannot be understated.

We will all need courage - courage to look at the reality before us and courage to respond with haste. I do not doubt God's eagerness to grant us all the tenacity and determination required.

Change

Curveballs

Most of us encounter a fair number of curveballs in the course of a lifetime. Curveballs are the challenging circumstances that come at us quick, usually when we least expect them. It's like being thrown a very fast, unpredictable pitch, but you forgot to bring a bat because you didn't even know you were playing baseball!

Divorce. Curveball. Cancer. Curveball. Layoff. Curveball. Death of a loved one. Curveball. You get the idea. And if I invited you to take a moment and list some of the most significant trials that have come your way, I have no doubt you could come up with at least a few.

As a pastor, I get to journey with people amidst the curveballs, and it is one of the most meaningful parts of the job.

Many would think that pastors would have all kinds of wonderful guidance to impart to individuals and families going through painful, awful experiences. But left to my own undeveloped insight, I come up lacking. Well, I guess there is one thing.

Curveballs stink.

Thankfully, pastors can depend on more than our own insights when tough times come. In fact, this doesn't just apply to pastors. We all can depend on a power that stretches far beyond our own: the love and guidance of God.

When we don't get it, when we're lost and upset and hurting, when we just want to trade in our own lives for a better one, we have a place to turn: our ever-present Creator. We can trust in the knowledge that God has promised to never leave us - ever - even in the moments we feel so very alone.

Sometimes, I have to read a Bible passage about 1.5 million times before it really sinks in. Lately I've been encountering Matthew 11:28-29 a lot. Jesus says: "Come to me all you that are weary and carrying heavy burdens, and I will give you rest. Take my yoke upon you and learn from me, for I am gentle and humble in heart, and you will find rest for your souls."

Rest. Jesus knew that when the really difficult stuff happens, what we often need most is rest, emotionally, physically, and spiritually.

When we need a personal encounter with that promised rest, there are a variety of places to go: a church family, a network of loved ones, a support group, or a peaceful afternoon at Quarry Hill Nature Center - one of my personal favorites. These are all places to experience an authentic connection to the sacred.

I don't know why curveballs enter our lives, but they do. There is grace in the fact that it is sometimes through the stinkiest of curveballs that we grow, learn, and develop the most.

When the baseball is coming in fast, and it's too late to adjust your swing, remember one thing: God is near and will never leave. When you hit the ball and when you don't. When the pitches come straight and when they take a curve. In and through all of it, God is at your side.

It's Not All Rainbows, Sparklers and Unicorns

Identity crisis. Global food crisis. Marriage crisis. Refugee crisis. Midlife crisis. There are a multitude of events that can take place which fit the definition of a crisis. According to dictionary.com, a crisis is "a stage in a sequence of events at which the trend of all future events, especially for better or for worse, is determined; turning point."

A crisis is a turning point. I generally think of a crisis as something inherently negative, but that isn't actually the case. Historically, my reflex is to turn away from them (and then run, as far and as fast as possible). But my wise friend Shelley expressed an alternative slant on the topic during our early morning walk last weekend. She shared the following quote: "Never waste a crisis."

I later searched for the origin of this quote and came up without a clear consensus. It has been attributed to Winston Churchill, M. F. Weiner, and Rahm Emmanuel. The quote likely goes back even farther in history and reflects deep, lasting truths about the true nature of crises.

A crisis can change the trajectory of a life, a community, a country, or even a whole planet - for worse OR for better. The idea of never wasting a crisis is rooted in the depth of their transformative nature. To waste a crisis is to waste an opportunity to make a shift, to miss out on a chance to reshape a trend, a pattern, or a behavior.

Don't get me wrong. It isn't all rainbows, sprinkles, and unicorns.

A crisis is often a terrible, painful, raw thing - and in the midst of it, a crisis can feel like anything other than an opportunity. A solution is rarely obvious at the outset.

But within this uncertainty and challenge there generally rests a kernel of possibility. If we can find a way to carefully harvest it, that kernel is pure potentiality. It is a ticket toward otherwise impossible realities that couldn't occur without the crisis at hand.

The Bible is full of examples of transformative crises - scenarios that initially appear terrible but become life-giving. In the Old Testament, a fellow named Jonah runs away from God and ends up getting swallowed whole by a giant fish. Some would call that a pretty significant crisis.

But through that swallowing and the events which follow, Jonah ends up regurgitated and prayerful - expressing words of trust in chapter two of his biblical book's namesake. By the end of the story, Jonah's life isn't perfect and neither is his attitude, but he has certainly learned a few things. That's the way it often is with a crisis. Our lives don't end up perfect, but we've changed.

The cross is another powerful example of the transformative potential of a crisis. Jesus' death was a profound crisis for his followers. The situation seemed hopeless. The emotional landscape for everyone who knew him appeared dry and desolate. But in that crisis remained a kernel of possibility, and that little kernel led to an empty tomb and a resurrected Christ. That little kernel reshaped the world.

"Never waste a crisis." I'm holding on tight to these words. They remind me that a crisis - no matter how big, hairy, or scary - is an opportunity, not an inevitable disaster.

Hibernating
on the Fence

Decision-making is an area of expertise for some. These dear people are able to make decisions large and small all while feeling calm and certain.

I ran into a woman last week in a waiting room who was talking about her career path. She had recently retired from teaching. "I just knew all along that I would be a teacher. I always knew," she said.

I have another friend who chose the location of his medical residency by drawing a slip of paper out of a hat, and he felt great about that approach.

Perhaps you have an innate sense of discernment. If so, I would like to follow you around for the next month and absorb a bit of your wisdom! Decision-making does not come as easily to me. The daily, small-scale decisions are no problem. I have no trouble choosing what to do on a Saturday afternoon or what to eat for supper.

The challenge for me is life's larger decisions. I don't just sit on the fence. I hibernate on it. I am perpetually plagued by a line in Robert Frost's poem, "The Road Not Taken:"

Two roads diverged in a wood,
and I — I took the one less traveled by,
and that has made all the difference.

It is unclear whether his choice of road was positive or negative. What did you mean, Mr. Frost? "All the difference" in a good way? Or "all the difference" in a bad way?

It often seems easier to simply sit still.

Another challenge in my decision-making approach is a tendency to wait for some kind of holy intervention. However, major God interruptions rarely happen for me. Sometimes I get a little nudge in my gut one way or the other but not usually. I've never seen the clouds in the sky develop into words and arrows pointing "THIS WAY" or "THAT WAY."

No, when it comes to life's bigger decisions, I generally wait and wait and wait until I absolutely have to make a decision. And then I worry whether it was the right one.

This is not an ideal approach.

We're all faced with ample decisions in life. Instead of turning into knots of angst and uncertainty, maybe it's better if we find ways to make clear choices and then move forward. Discernment is defined as the act of making a decision or judgment. At its best, discernment leads us through a process of prayer, seeking helpful counsel, making a decision, and then moving ahead.

Here are two bits of biblical guidance to help with your next decision-making experience:

John 14:16: "And I will ask the Father, and he will give you another Helper, to be with you forever."

Jesus said these words. They were originally meant to be a comfort to his disciples, but they're comforting for us, too. We're not alone. The Helper (that is, the Holy Spirit) is with us forever. FOREVER. Whatever the choice we're facing, there is comfort in knowing that we aren't alone. Even without God writing words of guidance in the sky, we can be assured that the Spirit is with us and never leaves us. The Helper walks with us and leads us into a process of healthy discernment.

Philippians 4:6-7: "Do not worry about anything, but in everything by prayer and supplication with thanksgiving let your requests be made known to God. And the peace of God, which surpasses all understanding, will guard your hearts and your minds in Christ Jesus."

On both ends of the discernment journey, it is our Creator's hope that we will pray and find peace in the promise that God hears us. God's peace surpasses all understanding.

Our human understanding is limited. But God's isn't. Whatever the roads we choose in life, it makes all the difference just to know that God will be there. Every choice and every path lead to the promise of God's presence.

May the next decision you face be an opportunity to experience a peace that surpasses all understanding.

Anniversaries of Loss

Birthdays and wedding anniversaries. Our Facebook feeds are full of such joyous occasions. We connect with one another on these special days by leaving encouragements online, sending greeting cards, and calling each other on the phone.

But what about the more difficult anniversaries? These happen each year as well, and many of us feel ill-equipped to acknowledge them in our own lives and in the lives of those we love.

"Anniversaries of loss" take many forms including the annual reminder of serious accidents, deaths, divorce finalizations, diagnoses, personal traumas and national disasters. Over the course of life, almost everyone experiences a loss that they are reminded of throughout the rest of their lives. This is part of being human. Since we can't escape loss, we can learn healthy coping methods which empower us to integrate such experiences into our personal narratives. Finding meaningful ways to acknowledge anniversaries of loss is one path toward reclaiming a sense of personal agency in a world where we sometimes feel helpless.

Acknowledge it

Some of us try to avoid acknowledging anniversaries of loss by burying the feelings and trying to think about something else. This usually doesn't work very well and can leave us feeling disconnected from our own sense of self and truth. An alternative approach is to acknowledge the anniversary of loss as well as the feelings it brings up. The word "acknowledge" means "to admit to be real or true." When it comes to painful annually reoccurring days, it can be a big, empowering step simply to admit to ourselves that we experienced something painful and we remember it every year (and we're often reminded of it other times of the year, too).

For some people, it is a very specific day that is connected to the loss. For others, it is a particular time of year. As it approaches, gently and lovingly notice how you feel. When we turn away from our feelings or ignore them, they often expand or come out later in a distorted way. But if we instead turn and look at them, the feelings often soften.

Extend yourself grace

Be gentle with yourself as you approach difficult anniversaries. Consider sharing about it with loved ones in a way that feels right for you. There is no rule that says you must talk about it, and there's no rule that you can't. Tune into your own sense of what's helpful to you.

Whether or not you share about the day with others, treat yourself with the utmost grace, love and compassion. Be good to your body, stay hydrated, and be patient with yourself. What you're going through is real and significant; your story and your experiences matter.

Notice gifts

One way that some people find meaning in loss is by exploring it for its gifts. Some losses feel too recent and painful for this. That's completely okay. Don't force yourself to make meaning in a situation that feels meaningless; life can be painful and senseless beyond words.

But for some experiences, there is meaning to be uncovered, and anniversaries of loss can be a good time to explore those gifts. What did the loss teach you about your own capacity for resilience? What did the deceased person help you to learn about life? How did the experience increase your empathy and understanding of other people? Mary Oliver has a poem called "The Uses of Sorrow" that goes like this:

Someone I loved once gave me
a box full of darkness.

It took me years to understand
that this, too, was a gift.

Anniversaries of loss can feel like a box full of darkness from the universe. Strangely and unexpectedly, however, within the box there can be gifts.

However you experience these annually reoccurring days, know that you are not alone and that you deserve to have peace in your life. May peace be yours as you integrate the realities of anniversaries of loss into your own story.

Funeral Orchids

My houseplants are surprisingly great spiritual teachers.

I never had plants or flowers or herbs in my house until I moved to Minnesota. I had been intimidated of owning anything that required watering. I was afraid I'd forget to care for them, and then their dry, drooping leaves would drop away and leave me feeling like a failure.

I've had to up my plant bravery since I became a pastor. The catalyst for this was when I started to receive them after funerals.

On funeral days at church, families are often inundated with plants. After the service, sometimes they have no idea what to do with them all. Often, they'd look to me, the pastor, and ask if I could give the plant a good home.

I love my funeral plants. In the midst of grief come these beautiful symbols of growth and perseverance. Beyond the general excitement of watching the plants thrive, they also teach life lessons.

Recently, my two orchids have taught me the most.

I received them last year about this time. I knew nothing about this special kind of plant. I heard one piece of advice from just about everyone: "Do not over-water them."

For the first month or two, the orchids kept their lovely blooms. The petals were dainty and delicate. Then the blooms fell off. I suspected it was normal, but I was still a little sad. I hoped that I hadn't killed my beloved orchids.

Over the next nine months, my orchids didn't do anything. They just soaked in the minimal water I gave them. The leaves and roots remained. Then, it happened. I saw a heavenly sight. Buds appeared on both orchids in the same week and blooms soon followed.

I was so happy when I noticed the first flower opening up that I invited everyone into my office to see. I also filled up my cell phone with flower photos.

Hope. That's what I see when I look at my orchids. I had no idea if they would ever bloom again, but they did.

Life is like an orchid sometimes. We have seasons. Sometimes we're blooming and everything is beautiful. Other times we go many months feeling spiritually or emotionally dormant.

Here's the amazing thing. Within the roots and stems of my houseplants, a force of renewal was always at work. Something was happening inside even when all I could see were leaves collecting dust on the window sill.

The same is true for human beings. We can't always see the forces at work in our souls, minds and hearts. We can't always feel how we're being nurtured, even in the midst of challenges. And then, in surprising ways, when we aren't expecting it, we start to notice little blooms within. Hope returns. And the God of love, who never left, remains.

The Compass

The "Maps and Diagrams" section of the Iowa Tests of Basic Skills was not my strong suit growing up. In fact, it was the portion I dreaded the most.

For most of my life, maps have seemed overwhelming and intimidating. Words, I love. But maps … there's just too much to take in.

Additionally, I'm not a person who has historically been known for being equipped with a natural sense of direction. GPS devices have been my close companions since they came into existence, getting me from Point A to Point B without much need for literal map-reading. I'd simply type in the address of my desired destination and go.

But times they are a-changin'. Hiking a multitude of trails up in Grand Marais last week inspired a new development: a love of maps and orienteering.

Standing on the trailhead of Lookout Mountain, I suddenly wondered, "Why do I keep telling myself that I'm bad with directions? Why do I still feel like seven-year-old Emily, who didn't excel at the Maps and Diagrams section of the Iowa Tests of Basic Skills? It's time to start telling myself a new story! I CAN read maps, and, in fact, I like it!"

And that brings me to my most exciting $3.99 purchase of all time: a compass! I purchased one at the Ben Franklin store in Grand Marais, and it just happens to have several amazing bonus features including a thermometer, whistle and looking glass (just in case I stumble upon a fascinating botanical specimen).

Where have you been all my life, compass?

Let me just say: hiking and map-reading are extra-enjoyable with a compass. It's the missing link. If, like me, you have ever felt directionally challenged, I have a tip: Buy a compass! You'll feel like a superhero with a super power. Just call me Direction Girl!

Up north, the air was fresh, the waves of Lake Superior were captivating and the waterfalls were invigorating. As I hiked along with my new compass, I realized that maybe there's a lot of stories I'm telling myself that aren't that helpful or true. Maybe I'm not so bad at map reading or directions. Maybe I just need the right tools!

Life is like that.

A lot of times, the challenges we face can be greatly remedied by the introduction of the right tools! Sometimes the right tool is as simple as an inexpensive compass. Sometimes the tool is an encouraging friend. A counselor. A weekly AA meeting. A new hobby. A book. A cup of coffee.

What are some old stories you're holding onto? Are there less-than-helpful measuring sticks you're still using to define your worth?

Remember Paul's words in his second letter to the Corinthians: "Therefore, if anyone is in Christ, the new creation has come: The old has gone, the new is here!"

Release those old stories and patterns you're still holding onto. Celebrate! The new has come. The old is gone. Grab a compass; let's explore.

Goodbye, House

There is a certain sweetness about finding a place to call home.

It was back in 1823 when actor and writer John Howard Payne penned the lyrics "Home! Sweet, sweet home! There's no place like home" for his musical *Clari*. Then Judy Garland made the words famous again in the 1939 film *The Wizard of Oz*, when she played the role of a young woman desperate to get back to Kansas.

I concur with Payne and Garland. There's no place like home sweet home. Yet home is not confined to one specific building, zip code, or area code. That's good news because the average American moves 12 times throughout their life.

Last weekend I moved from Stewartville into Rochester and transitioned from renter to first-time homeowner. The house in Stewie was the longest I'd ever lived in the same place. After nearly eight years, I had grown quite attached to the hilltop views, the sunrises, the sunsets, and the marvelous stargazing opportunities. But it wasn't just the sights that endeared it to me, but everything the home represented.

When I first pulled off Interstate 90 from Chicago to Stewartville it was the end of July, 2009. I was fresh out of seminary and a bit like a baby fawn taking her first pastoral steps. The house I rented was a sanctuary while I transitioned from graduate student to grownup. I could always be myself at home and never needed to pretend. That was a gift.

Since then, I've become a full-fledged adult, and the hardest work I've done in the last eight years has been the work that's taken place within. Like a hot air balloon pilot, God has been cutting the ropes that tied me to other people's expectations and judgments. In releasing me from those cords, I've been freed to find my true voice and launch. Having a safe space to call home has been priceless through this journey. I am deeply grateful for what has been my home sweet home - and for the people who provided encouragement, love and acceptance along the way.

Now, surrounded by stacks of boxes in the new abode, I begin a new season. Though I'll certainly miss the old place, a sense of blissful anticipation permeates my spirit. Justin and I found this new place together. This summer we'll get married and he'll move north from his current home in Iowa. I'm excited to make this house a home together - to garden, to laugh with our neighbors, to pay bills and mend fences and go on dates to Menards.

Pulling out of the old driveway for the last time was bittersweet. Justin was driving and I was tearing up. "Goodbye, house," I said one last time.

I don't think the house's response was audible to anyone else, but I just may have heard a faint, "Thanks for coming," as we headed north on Highway 63 toward our new home sweet home.

You

Love Yourself

L oving ourselves isn't optional. It's commanded by God. But in or-der to realize this, we have to carefully read and digest Jesus' words.

The Ten Commandments are outlined in the 20th chapter of the book of Exodus, and they teach us how to live in relationship with God and others. But God's guidance isn't limited to the Ten Commandments. The Old Testament is full of laws that helped early people of faith in the building of a just, life-giving society.

Fast forward a couple thousand years, and Jesus is presented with a question from an expert in the law (the story is found in Matthew 22:34-40 and Mark 12:28-34). The man asks, "Of all the laws, which is most important?" It is a great question, and Jesus responds with an excellent answer.

First, Jesus describes the most important commandment of all: "Love the Lord your God with all your heart and with all your soul and with all your mind and with all your strength." Jesus, well-versed in all of the Old Testament, recalls this command from Deuteronomy 6:4-5.

Then, it's time for the second most important commandment, which Jesus recalls from Leviticus 19:18, "Love your neighbor as yourself."

Bingo! Love your neighbor as YOURSELF. In order for this whole operation to work, we all have to love ourselves. Because if we don't love ourselves, it's going to be nearly impossible to love our neighbors.

When originally expressing the importance of loving our neighbors, God started from the basic premise that human beings were going to love themselves. Our Creator was assuming that all of us were going to remember that we were created in the image of God. Astounding! Amazing!

I can see why God didn't think we'd have trouble loving ourselves. Through the power of the Holy Spirit, the author of the universe lives within us, and what's not to love about that? But sadly, we often forget and disconnect from God at work within and among us. And when we do that, loving ourselves becomes harder and harder. We get buried under the weight of our mistakes, regrets, comparisons, and fears. We've all been there. In fact, most of us spend time there every day.

I wonder sometimes if the root of many of our local, national, and global concerns is the same: lack of respect and love for self. Turn on the news. Read a newspaper. It takes only a moment to recognize that our world is full of people who don't even like themselves, let alone love themselves. And it's wreaking havoc on a world that God created to be a place of goodness, mercy, and compassion.

Yet there is always hope. The tide can turn, and we can be part of that movement. We can be leaders in loving ourselves knowing that by doing so we are more able to love others.

Loving ourselves is more than a random theme from the library's self-help section. It's not mushy-gushy talk. It's the Gospel. To love ourselves is to take Jesus seriously in his invitation to help God build a healthy, peaceful world.

Wake up each day and say, "I am a loved and claimed child of God, and nothing will separate me from this truth." Model this for others. Find ways every day to nurture this sacred seed of love, and be wary of anything that might squelch its growth.

Valuing ourselves is not about building inflated self-confidence. It's about following one of the central commands of Christ. If we want to be patient with others, we must be patient with ourselves. If we want to be forgiving of others, we must be forgiving of ourselves.

Our Creator believes in our ability to love God, love ourselves, and love our neighbors. Let us go forth into the week ahead ready to love abundantly.

Be Yourself

As part of the journey toward becoming a Lutheran pastor, there's a process called candidacy that coincides with a graduate school experience called seminary. One of the initial phases of candidacy is that all potential pastors are required to receive a psychological exam.

It's a valuable step in the process and a way to ensure that prospective pastors have worked through their own life journeys to the point where it is safe for them to accompany others along the way. I was a few months into my seminary classwork in Chicago when it was time for my psychological exam.

I was fairly convinced I had it all together at that point. I imagined I'd spend a quick Saturday going through the psychological exam and be on my merry way. A few standardized tests, a visit with a counselor... end of story.

Then the day arrived. The Minneapolis-area counselor and his intern invited me to share a bit about myself, and so I did. He asked questions, and I answered them all with a smile and some version of, "But it all worked out for the best, and I learned so much along the way."

And then he paused and with a softened smile offered a generous, life-changing gift, "Emily, you don't have to prove anything to me. You don't have to be anything other than who you are. I know that there must be at least some hurt behind these life experiences, and that's

OK. I have no expectations of you."

I cried for two days.

It has taken ten years to understand the depth of the gift that counselor gave me. He was offering me a particular kind of freedom. A freedom to just be myself. To feel what I feel. To stop trying to prove my worth to anyone and everyone by being as palatable as possible.

As I glanced through the initial chapters of the Gospel of Luke a few days ago in preparation for the week ahead, I noticed God offers a similar kind of freedom to people. Everyone in the Christmas story arrives by a different path. Joseph, Mary, the shepherds, they all come with different feelings and experiences.

Mary starts out "perplexed" (see 1:29). The shepherds see an angel and are initially "terrified" (see 2:9). When the shepherds arrive to find Mary, Joseph, and baby Jesus, they are elated and end up "glorifying and praising" God (see 2:20). But Mary expresses her emotional state differently, and she has the freedom to do so. We're told she spends time "pondering" it all in her heart (see 2:19).

Throughout the story, people get to feel how they feel. God doesn't posit a list of requirements and expectations to Mary, Joseph, and the shepherds. God gives them freedom to authentically soak it all in.

As we approach the manger in the days ahead, may we, too, remember that freedom. Freedom to come as we are and be who we are without the weight of unnecessary expectations.

Oh come, let us adore him.

Loudly or quietly.

With bold joy or reflective contemplation.

By candlelight or Christmas tree lights.

Gift eternal.

Christ the Lord.

Your Real, Whole Self

In the weeks leading up to the first day of seventh grade, I was plagued by anxiety nightmares in which I was perpetually lost in the school building. I was always running late - well past the ringing of the tardy bell - and just when I thought I'd made it to the right classroom, I'd find myself going up and down the stairs again and again unable to find the correct doorway.

If I were to summarize the last five weeks of my adult life, I'd say it was like those dreams. I was lost and none of the entrances seemed to be correct. It was a maze of hospital stays, blood tests (35 in total), and platelet-related drama.

It was a bad sort of dream. Only I was awake. I could tell you it all led to a profound spiritual awakening, but that would be false. The truth: It stunk, and I'm seriously considering redoing the entire summer. So if you have any sort of magical backwards-moving clock, let me know. I'd be glad to swing by and pick it up.

John Mayer has a song called "3x5." In it, he sings, *Maybe I'll tell you all about it when I'm in the mood to lose my way with words.* That's how I feel about the summer of 2015. I could talk more about it, but it's all becoming a blur.

Also, when I think about it too much, I get a giant lump in my throat. It comes from some combination of overwhelming sadness that there is so much suffering in our universe and overwhelming gratitude that there is so much beauty and goodness. It's enough to cause me to completely lose my words and sit in tears because God is simultaneously so very mysterious and so very compassionate.

That's the general backstory on the hiatus I took from the column. I was really sick, then I was healing, and now I'm back. Thanks for waiting! Hopefully the worst has passed. I'm certainly banking on the idea that the best is yet to come.

While I was healing, I did some thinking about this column's title. "The Lady Pastor" fit nicely for the past four years. It was my nickname among the volunteer chaplains group in southern Illinois during my internship year in 2007. It was a nickname I initially resented, but then found a way to embrace. But something about it doesn't feel quite right anymore. It's like the favorite sweater that one day starts to feel itchy and uncomfortable.

I think these intense medical and emotional experiences have inspired me to think in some different ways about life, purpose and healing. I've decided I just want to focus on being my real self from now on. Not the platelet patient, or the Lady Pastor, or the people pleaser, or the perfectionist, or any other subset of my identity. Just myself. Fully Emily, sans any itchy sweaters.

Thank you for accepting me just as I am. I hope you can extend that same grace to yourself. I hope that you, too, can honor exactly who you are and who you are becoming. Fully. Without judgment. Without shame. With total, complete acceptance.

Sometimes we spend a lot of life trying to be what we think other people need or want us to be. It's a dangerous path, and if you're on it, please join me in turning back. Just be YOU. Your real, whole self.

"Holy Everything," the column's new title, represents an approach to life. It is a way to acknowledge the world around us. It is to live as if there is something sacred wrapped up in all our days and experiences. The content will be generally the same, with a focus on wonder, curiosity, spirituality and faith.

I hope we can continue to journey together. From what I can see from this new vantage point, the view up ahead looks promising. The doors are starting to open, and together, maybe we won't get quite so lost.

You Are You

A chronic illness is defined as a condition which lasts for a long period of time and which generally cannot be cured. According to the Centers for Disease Control, about half of all adults in the US (nearly 150 million people) have one or more chronic health conditions.

Half! That's a big bunch of people!

We all know people who are managing conditions they'll probably have for the rest of their lives. Perhaps you are swimming in those waters yourself - discerning which treatment plan to choose or dealing with medication side effects or trying to get in to see a specialist. If that's the case, remember that you are not alone.

Adapting to life with a chronic illness has unique and important spiritual implications. I naively thought that by this point in my own medical journey with a chronic autoimmune condition, I'd have it figured out. I imagined I'd have made peace with it all: God and the doctors and my own body. But... not so much. Instead I've come to recognize that the path toward peace is lifelong. Still, here are a few bits of guidance I've picked up on my journey with a chronic illness:

1. Give yourself a heaping measure of grace. If you have a chronic illness or you're the caregiver, be extra nice to yourself - even when you're acting weird. You're doing the best you can, and that's all anyone can ask of you. You're going to lose your temper sometimes. You're going to be in a bad mood now and then - maybe for weeks on end. You might get irrational and tired and bossy. It's okay. Forgive yourself. Apologize when appropriate and then move on. Your body and your brain are doing the best they can with the cards they've been dealt.

2. It's okay if your feelings about God change with time. There might be moments when you feel like everything happens for a reason. And there might be moments when you feel like there is no rhyme or reason to anything. There might be times when God feels really close. And there might be times when God feels really far away. There might be days when you can clearly see the gifts of your illness. And there might be days when you curse life itself because you hate your illness so much. These are all valid feelings. Let them flow through you like clouds through the sky. You don't need to get attached to any specific feeling. Just let them come and let them go.

3. Feel disappointment without getting stuck there. Sometimes when dealing with a chronic illness, you feel like you need to convince yourself that you're happy even when you're not. You say things like, "Well, it's really not that bad," or "It could be worse," or "I really shouldn't complain." You do everything possible to avoid the actual emotion you are experiencing which is often disappointment. You're legitimately disappointed because you'd like to be able to do the things you used to do, or make plans the way you used to make plans, or move the way you used to move. I have found that giving myself permission to simply feel the disappointment loosens it up so I can keep going. It is possible (and even healthy) to experience disappointed feelings without getting stuck in that emotional state.

4. Remember you are not your diagnosis. You are you. First and foremost, you are a loved, unique, important person. You are also a person with a medical diagnosis. But YOU are not your diagnosis. You're still you. There are times when it's hard to remember this distinction - the difference between you and the terms in your medical chart - but try. Try to remember that your diagnosis is only one part of the functioning of your body. Your diagnosis is only one slice of your life pie. There are seasons in life when that slice gets all the attention. But there are other seasons when the other slices of your pie (your hobbies, your loved ones, your beautiful eyes, your compassionate heart, your job) deserve attention, too. You are not your diagnosis.

Jesus once said, "I came that they may have life and have life abundant." I believe Jesus meant this for all people regardless of the breadth and depth of their medical file. If you or someone you love has been diagnosed with a chronic condition, may you experience love, peace, and life abundant - all along the way.

Look Up and Jump Out

The word "should" is commonplace. It is so frequently used that it often fades into the background of our shared vernacular. It appears at first to be a wallflower standing alongside "also," "that," and "many."

But should is not so naïve or innocent. It's actually a very powerful word, and it can be dangerous, too.

I hear "should" a lot in conversations about health, faith, and human relationships.

- I should eat more vegetables.
- We should go to church more often.
- She should really start exercising.
- He should spend more time at home.

"Should" is a heavy word, and it often comes with a few loads of baggage. Baggage in the form of guilt, judgment, and shame. When we do things in life purely because we - or someone else - think we should, the outcome is often less than stellar. "Should" is not a great long-term motivator.

Instead, "should" is often the sweet refrain of complacency. The more we use the word, the more complacent we become. It's not a great cycle.

A scenario: You wake up thinking "I should exercise today." You don't necessarily have any real plans to do so, but you know deep inside that you want to. But by evening, you haven't. You go to bed thinking, "I really should've exercised today." You feel guilt, self-condemnation, and shame. You wake up feeling the same way.

"Should" didn't do you any favors.

I was recently at the salon and happened to overhear someone talking about her involvement in a faith community. Looking down, she hesitantly said, "I don't go to church, but I know I should."

The overarching sentiment wasn't excitement or joy about exploring a life of faith. It was guilt about not going to church on Sunday mornings. Now, I'm certain the Holy Spirit was already at work in her life in a host of ways. For example, I could see she was extremely bright and creative. But it was probably pretty hard to recognize all those things worth celebrating because she was stuck so far in a haunting hole of all the things she thought she should be.

We've all been there. Everyone gets stuck in a "should" hole sometimes, desperately wanting a way out, but not sure how to get there. So we retreat to saying "we should." It becomes our common refrain. And while we think it's helping us, it isn't. We're setting ourselves up to feel bad.

There's another way. We've got a language full of alternative words to use in describing routines and behaviors we'd like to incorporate into our lives. Next time you catch yourself using the word "should," I invite you to pause.

Ask yourself: Do I really mean it? If not, maybe I could let this idea go. But if I do mean it, how might I make that happen? Are there steps I could take today to propel me from "should" to "will?" Incorporate other words and phrases when possible - phrases which better represent how you feel. Things like: "might," "will consider," and "could possibly."

Unpack your use of "should." Set yourself up to feel good and encouraged whenever you can. Use words in ways that give you and the people around you the best chance at success.

If you happen to get stuck inside the deep, dark "should" hole, remember that you can always look up and jump out! There is light and possibility all around, and the Holy Spirit is always ready to remind you of your infinite worth.

The Unconventional Bear

Most of my memories of kindergarten are hazy, but there are still a few that I hold close to my heart.

There was the moment I finally learned to tie my shoes. And there was the moment when my sweetheart, Andrew, kissed me on the cheek under the playground bridge.

But even more than those, I remember the time I colored outside the lines.

Nap time had just ended, and the classroom was still a little dim. Everyone was working on the same coloring sheet. It was a bear. A happy, cartoon bear. My train of thought as a curious five-year-old was something like, "I think this bear needs fur."

I first colored the inside of the bear completely, then I added short brown crayon strokes all along the edge, so it resembled something like a poky layer of fuzz.

When my teacher walked by, she was not pleased with what she saw. "Emily, you must stay inside the lines. You'll have to start again." Mortified with my mistake, I made no attempt to explain whatever strange inspiration had overtaken me. I began again and vowed to do it right.

My teacher was a caring woman who nurtured generations of children during her tenure. She was probably right in correcting my furry bear, but I wish she hadn't. I sometimes wish that instead of a lesson in the importance of following the rules, I had learned a lesson in the value of creativity that day.

Following the rules has always come pretty easily to me. The struggle is that I am often so inclined to conform and obey that I forget to leave room to explore, create and fail.

I think there are many of us in this same boat.

We want to do and be our very best, so we avoid mistakes. We stick with what's familiar. We figure out the rules and then do all we can to follow them. But in that process, there's a little flame that often gets squelched - the flame of everything that's possible.

There's room for both bears in the forest of this life. There's a place for the perfectly groomed bear composed of all that's tried and true and trusted. And there's plenty of room for the unconventional bear with a funny haircut and lots of new ideas.

In a rapidly changing world, we need the gifts of both kinds of bears. Sometimes life invites us to conform and sometimes life invites us to create. But no matter what the future holds, we never need to be afraid of a little fur.

Us

We Need Help

It was a weekend of fun, food and a giant, flaming pile of wood. My husband, Justin, and I recently spent a few days in Iowa for the annual Stoll family bonfire at his parents' farm. There are many reasons to enjoy bonfire weekend (the many varieties of chips and dip, for example), but of all the delights, quality playtime with our nephews and niece is at the top of my list.

Sophia is fearless and kind. Her big brothers, Conner and Max, are creative, thoughtful and full of energy. The three of them together are a trifecta of merriment. Relatives and friends are elated at the mere sight of their cuteness and curiosity. I'm grateful to be their Auntie Em.

During bonfire weekend, the kids and I enjoyed nature walks, treehouse time, and variations of imaginary school, restaurant and house.

Sophia, age three, has reached a stage where she is now very willing to ask for help. "Em-a-wee, I need you," she said emphatically and often.

Each time she requested assistance, I paused and pondered for a moment. She made it look so easy to ask for help. She is a very independent young person, but Sophia recognizes what many adults have forgotten along the way: life is a lot more enjoyable and manageable when we ask for help.

We all benefit when this kind of attitude takes root in our homes, businesses, schools, churches and government offices. To ask for help takes courage and humility. It is to admit we are imperfect. It is to accept that we are not all-knowing or all-powerful.

The help we need takes many forms. Sometimes we're like Sophia, and we need tangible help — getting on the swing or picking up groceries or bringing over cold medicine. Other times, the help we need is less concrete but just as immediate and important — someone to talk to after a death, a solution to a load of financial debt that feels insurmountable, a way out of an oppressive job or relationship. In all these cases, we need help, and we need each other. We need to be able to say to other human beings, "I need you."

As important as it is to be able to ask for assistance, it's just as important to be willing to be the helpers! Are we willing to hear each other's requests for help? Our compassionate willingness to respond individually and collectively to the needs of others is paramount to nurturing healthy communities and a just planet.

We are better together than we are individually. We can help each other; we can be there for each other. It takes courage to ask, and it takes courage to respond.

Thank you, wise Sophia (whose name, coincidentally, means wisdom in Greek) for paving the way.

Accidentally Imprinted

I was at the MacBride Raptor Project in Iowa with my significant other, Justin, admiring more than 20 birds of prey. All the birds there have been rescued, and none of them can live independently in the wild.

I became interested in falconry last fall and have since been fascinated by eagles, owls, and hawks. The MacBride Raptor Project, also called the Raptor Center, was a perfect Saturday afternoon adventure for a falcon fan.

All the birds there had plaques outside their cages listing their name, species, and how they ended up at the Raptor Center. On a number of the signs were the words *accidentally imprinted*.

"What on earth does that mean?" I asked Justin. "How does one accidentally imprint a bird? I understand imprinting but I don't understand how it could be accidental."

Imprinting refers to a sensitive period of time right after a young animal is born. During the imprinting phase, the new animal recognizes its parent and begins to bond.

After a bit of research, I learned that the accidental imprinting of raptors and other animals is not entirely uncommon. It happens anytime someone interferes with the bonding process between a new animal and its parent. Accidental imprinting can have serious ramifications, as animals are often not accepted back into their families after the separation occurs.

Nearly a month has now passed since I met Orion, Cyprus, Asia, Spirit, Isabow and the rest of the raptor pack. The words "accidentally imprinted" became glued inside my mind that day and have been rolling around ever since. Perhaps my new avian friends left a permanent imprint on me!

My ponderings have led me to this conclusion: Accidental imprinting is not a phenomenon limited to raptors, ducks, and bison (as tragically occurred recently in Yellowstone). Humans do it, too - perhaps with even greater ramifications.

We imprint our attitudes, fears, biases and opinions. We also imprint our hopes and dreams. We carry all this stuff with us every day, and then, often unknowingly, we imprint other people with it.

Sometimes this imprinting is good. We imprint the people around us with our love, acceptance, forgiveness, and compassion. Other times, our imprinting is not so good. We imprint our friends, parents, kids, grandkids, co-workers, and total strangers with all of our toxic run-off. We don't necessarily mean to, but it happens nevertheless; and just as we are imprinting on others, they are imprinting on us.

Like a seal into hot wax, we're all imprinting one another - sealing our moods, perspectives, and attitudes onto the people around us.

We accidentally imprint as individuals and we also do it as institutions - businesses, congregations, and political parties. This will always be the case. Humans are social creatures. We influence one another and that won't change. What can change is the intentionality with which we approach our imprinting.

Every interaction, every memo, every television interview, every mealtime conversation - they are all opportunities to imprint compassion. But we have to choose it! When we witness unhealthy imprinting taking place in our homes, churches, and places of work, we must find the courage to confront it.

We can be sanctuaries for each other. Like the Raptor Center in Iowa, we, too, can create safe spaces. We all need those sanctuaries because we all have wounds from the accidental imprinting we've experienced along the journey of life.

Together, we get to build a world full of sanctuaries - one brick at a time.

God Is Love

The time has come for overpriced assortments of candy and flowers, last-minute dinner reservations, and highly sugared classroom parties.

Valentine's Day is right around the corner. While some folks are quick to criticize good ol' V-Day for being utterly commercialized, I'm happy to admit that I'm still a fan. As a child, my appreciation for the day generally revolved around the prospect of gleaning the attention (and candy-grams) of Andrew (in kindergarten), Jess (in first grade), Eric (in fifth grade), and the rest of my elementary school crushes.

As an adult, my focus has shifted. Now I like celebrating Valentine's Day for the same reason that I like officiating weddings: Love gets center stage! In a world that is desperate for a true, deepened understanding of love, every February a whole day gets devoted to the concept. Bonus: We get to discern for ourselves where we want to direct the spotlight of our Valentine's attention.

February 14th doesn't have to be about manufacturing visions of a super adoring spouse or significant other. It doesn't have to be about overly hyped expectations or overly priced date nights. Instead, Valentine's Day can just as easily be a chance to celebrate love in all its forms: love between family, friends, colleagues, and fellow church members. Most especially, why not approach Valentine's Day as the perfect opportunity to celebrate the love of God?

I recognize God's love is not the traditional focus of Valentine's Day. But maybe it should be, because God's love provides the roots and the life force of every other form of love we'll ever experience.

So I'm here to proclaim: whether you have a sweetie or not, whether you have a secret admirer or not, whether your spouse remembers to get you a card or not: Valentine's Day is still for you. Because you're loved. You are incredibly, eternally, unequivocally loved by your Creator. So let's celebrate!

I studied British literature in college and read more sonnets and love poems than I could ever hope to retain. There are many brilliant writers, filmmakers, and artists who have found a multitude of ways to describe the complexities of love.

The Holy Spirit also inspired some great love material in the pages of Scripture. Here are a few of my favorite passages in the Bible written specifically about the love of God.

• **Lamentations 3:22-23:** "The steadfast love of the Lord never ceases; his mercies never come to an end; they are new every morning; great is your faithfulness."

God's love is permanent and never-ceasing. Each new day is a fresh chance to be reminded of the permanence of our Creator's love.

• **John 3:16-17:** "For God so loved the world that he gave his only Son, so that everyone who believes in him may not perish but may have eternal life. Indeed, God did not send the Son into the world to condemn the world, but in order that the world might be saved through him."

Perhaps the most beloved verses of the Bible! God desired that the whole world might be saved and brought to a new understanding of love through Jesus. Thank you, Lord, for loving us so much.

• **1 John 4:8-12** (selected portions): "For God is love. God's love was revealed to us in this way: God sent his only Son into the world so that we might live through him. In this is love, not that we loved God but that he loved us...if we love one another, God lives in us."

These verses get right at the heart of many of our deepest faith questions. Who is God? Where is God? What does God think/feel/

say/do? The verse states, "God is love." God is love. And God loved and chose us. What a sacred gift!

May your Valentine's Day be full of authentic, deeply rooted love!

Finn, the Dog

I am judgmental. Finn is not. He's my fiancé's dog. Finn is the least judgmental creature I have known, and he's shown me a lot of mercy lately.

Pets are often like that. Slow to anger and abounding in love.

I grew up with an outdoor dog and I'm allergic to cats, so my exposure to indoor animals is limited (other than Sandy the Childhood Hamster and Thumper the Childhood Rabbit).

Justin, on the other hand, grew up with many indoor pets. He's had Finn the Redbone Coonhound for about a year and a half. As Justin and I have gotten closer to marriage and living in the same home, my anxiety about having an indoor pet has increased.

I've had a lot of judgments in my heart toward Finn. Judgments like: He's going to make messes. He's going to be naughty. He's going to be inconvenient. He's going to bark at the neighbors.

My judgments aren't based in reality (most judgments aren't). They are based on my overactive imagination - a mix of stereotypes and anxieties and all my worst fears.

A couple weeks ago, Finn came over for his first visit to the new place. I was convinced that he was going to destroy my home.

But, as it turns out, Finn didn't destroy anything. Instead, he showed me compassion. Even though I was afraid he'd be my nemesis, he treated me like his new best friend.

Eager for walks and pats on the back, he didn't care that I had judged him so unfairly. My anxiety melted away as he insisted on repeatedly climbing into my lap to give me "Finn hugs": a special kind of embrace that only a 70-pound dog can give.

I can't believe I get to have such a dear man and a dear dog in my life - both so very merciful to me. It's the best two-for-one deal I can imagine.

Judgment, whether toward pets or people or situations or political parties, takes up a lot of emotional space. When something displeases us in any way, we tend to immediately pick it apart and dismiss it.

This instinct toward judgment serves no meaningful purpose other than to draw make-believe lines in the sand between us and them, insiders and outsiders, good and bad. Judgment builds walls; mercy builds bridges. Jesus directed his followers away from judgment and instead pointed them toward mercy.

In Luke 6:36, Jesus said, "Be merciful, just as your Father is merciful." In the next verse, he continued, "Do not judge, and you will not be judged; do not condemn and you will not be condemned. Forgive, and you will be forgiven."

In spite of people's past transgressions, Jesus on many occasions proclaimed, "Your sins are forgiven." That was mercy. A Samaritan man dropped everything to help a terribly injured person in Luke 10. That was mercy. A father joyfully welcomed home his young, far-straying son in Luke 15, and that, too, was mercy.

To delay judgment, to respond with kindness, to choose building a bridge over building a wall - these are expressions of mercy. They are transformative for the giver and receiver. As Jesus encouraged in Luke 10:37, may we also "go and do likewise."

The Greatest Joy

Last Saturday Justin and I got married. It was blissful. Our immediate family accompanied us for the day, and the 12 of us had loads of love-filled fun. We laughed. We smiled for photos. We made vows in a garden full of wildflowers and butterflies. Our brothers signed a piece of paper as our witnesses.

Now we are wed.

The morning of our nuptials, my sister-in-law, Sweta, lovingly asked what kinds of things I'd been dreaming about for my wedding day since I was a little girl. I shared with her that I hadn't. A wedding and a marriage weren't realities I'd thought about much - as a little girl or as an adult woman.

Then I met Justin, and we connected at a point in my life when 1) I was willing to invest whole-heartedly in a relationship with a safe and loving person and 2) I was willing to let a compassionate partner care about me without running away from that love.

From there, the pieces fell into place. My life, like all other lives, hasn't been a fairy tale. Justin is not a perfect prince, and he didn't sweep me off my feet and fix everything that was broken in my life. I am not a perfect princess, and I haven't made all his dreams instantly come true.

Instead, we're two compatible humans who said, "This is a good thing. Let's commit to sticking with it." I said to him, "You are brilliant and fun and respectful. Also I like how you make things out of wood." He said, "You are kind. I like your words. You're the strongest person I've ever met."

What I love about us most is that we bring out good things in one another. I hope that's always the case.

My brother, Josh, says one of the keys to happiness is to have few expectations. I used to laugh that his approach wasn't optimistic enough, but now I think it's brilliant. It is a perspective which admits that there are many things outside one's own control.

Justin and I didn't have excessive expectations for our wedding. We wanted to be with our parents, siblings, nephews and niece. That was about it. We figured the rest would be a bonus.

It was.

Spending the morning with my mom and sister-in-law: bonus. Planting a tree with our parents and watching each of our guests add in another scoopful of earth: bonus. Dancing on the back porch and eating cheesecake while the kids played with bubble wands until bedtime: bonus. Staying up to wash dishes with my partner at the end of the day and repeatedly calling each other "husband" and "wife" just to try on the new titles: bonus. Justin got me a gratitude journal for our first Christmas; my entry for August 5th was very long.

We ended our vows with the line, "To love you and be loved by you is my greatest joy and privilege." Justin and I are at the very beginning of this partnership journey. We both have a lot to learn, and we'll be learning it together. We'll make loads of mistakes. We'll grow and change.

Thankfully, we won't learn how to be married in isolation. We'll do it surrounded by a network of family and friends who have always been quick to extend unconditional support. Their love, we both recognize, is the biggest bonus of them all.

Don't Spoil Beauty of this Place

Visiting Kolkata, India, in mid-January was transformative; the experience was disorienting and reorienting at the same time. Kolkata expanded my understanding of beauty.

I was in India to attend the wedding of my brother, Josh, and his wife, Sweta. My mom and I made the journey together. The six-day trip included several days of meaningful marriage rituals and one day of exploring the city.

Our time in India moved swiftly. Now that I'm back, I sometimes find myself wondering if it really happened. Was it all a dream? A colorful, vibrant, surprising wondrous figment of my imagination?

But the photos on my laptop and the henna-stains on my hands remind me it all really happened.

On our sightseeing day in Kolkata, a group of us visited a park. At the entrance was a sign on behalf of the city park association: *Don't Spoil Beauty of this Place.*

It was meant to encourage visitors to pick up their trash and express general respect for the place. But the sign has since become my mantra. Seek beauty; don't spoil it.

There are so many tempting ways to spoil beauty. It isn't just about litter and garbage. It's also about the rubbish that happens on our insides, too - all the ways we spoil reality with our judgments, regrets, insecurities and fixations.

A harsh word.

Contagious negativity.

Hopelessness.

Condescension.

The author of Psalm 27 writes, "One thing I ask from the Lord, this only do I seek: that I may dwell in the house of the Lord all the days of my life, to gaze on the beauty of the Lord."

The Psalmist's prayer is to gaze upon God's beauty all the days of his life. That's my prayer, too.

In India, I witnessed people embracing God's beauty through ritual and dance and conversation. Through shared meals. Through walks in the park, selfies with strangers, and brightly colored sarees.

The Hebrew word for beauty used by the author of Psalm 27 is *noam*. It means kindness, delightfulness, goodness, and pleasantness.

To gaze upon God's beauty is to recognize kindness at work in the world and delight in it. That's what happened to me in India. I experienced the kindness of God, and it was beautiful.

Sitting beside by mom for about 40 hours of airplane time: beauty.

Some of the cousins smeared tumeric on the faces of all the women in attendance with the words, "We are all family now." That was beauty, too.

The millennia-old marriage rituals: beauty.

The total bliss of my brother the moment he saw his wife before the final ceremony: beauty.

Meeting my brother's new mother, father, and grandmother and getting to spend time with much of my sister-in-law's family tree: beauty.

One of Sweta's uncles pulled my mom and me onto the dance floor with the words, "This is your one chance. You must dance!" That was beauty.

In every aspect of the experience there existed another invitation to gaze upon the beauty of God. To see it. To admire it. To savor it.

Don't spoil beauty of this place. That sign in the park in Kolkata provided more than a useful sanitary suggestion. It was wisdom - pure and true.

Thank you, India, for all your wondrous beauty.

She Was My Girl

Justin celebrated a birthday earlier this month, and we checked out a few estate sales as part of the merriment. At our second stop, Justin stayed in the garage exploring the massive collection of tools while I stepped inside. There was art on every wall and card tables full of trinkets, stationery, napkins, and books.

The first box I noticed was full of eyeglasses. There were dozens of pairs each with a different prescription. On the wall was a Norman Rockwell-style painting of an eye doctor and his patient.

The story of the home was beginning to take shape. It appeared an optometrist had lived there.

Walking from room to room was thrilling. There were treasures everywhere, and just being near them made me feel as if I had won an unannounced lottery.

In the dining room were beautiful pieces of pottery, serving trays, mint-condition cutlery, and china sets from around the world. On walls and shelves, there were wooden sculptures like pieces I'd seen from Tanzania.

It felt like I had stepped into a novel. As Detective Emily, my task was to piece all the clues together. An eye doctor. People who liked to entertain. Travelers.

Heading upstairs

I sent a text to Justin, "Heading upstairs." He was down exploring the basement.

As I stepped into the first bedroom, the excitement continued. The closets were full of vintage clothing: gloves and hats and blouses - all exquisite.

Who was this woman? I wondered.

In the second bedroom, I noticed a most magnificent collection of belts with styles spanning at least 40 years. Some were bright and bold, others were soft and neutral. They were all beautiful.

Justin and I left that afternoon without purchasing much, but we discussed coming back the following day when everything was 50 percent off. That evening, while Justin chaperoned a college dance, I read up on vintage belts and dreamed about the life and travels of the people who had once lived in that house.

Day two

We returned early the next day. There were more blank spaces on the walls; much of the artwork had been purchased, but I didn't mind. I hadn't come for the artwork. I came back to sit in the room with those belts. I just wanted to see them and soak in the life of the woman who wore them.

There was another estate sale explorer in the room with me. She was trying on one of the coats for sale, a red one. "I might get it," she said. "Verna had the most amazing style."

"You knew her?" I asked; the detective had a fresh lead.

"Yes, I lived down the street. I was friends with George and Verna's kids. I'm back in town for the weekend visiting my sister." She headed down the hall to another room, but she had given me more of the story. Now I had a name: Verna.

I looked down at the box of belts and picked up my favorite for the hundredth time. It had been an accessory to dinners, travels, and evenings with friends. It wasn't so much that I wanted to buy it. It was more like I wanted to absorb the stories of which it took part.

Hello, George

I was still with the belts when a man entered who looked to be in his mid-80s. It was clear he wasn't another estate sale buyer. This was the optometrist and homeowner, George. The keeper of all the stories I'd been imagining since the previous afternoon. His eyes were red and puffy.

"My Verna had such class. Such style," he said to me.

"She sure did," I said. "I've never seen such beautiful belts." I paused, aware that as I stood touching Verna's things, it was more than a personal treasure hunt. For George, I was in the museum of his life, and everything deserved the utmost care.   '

"I'm Emily," I said and shook his hand.

"I'm George," he said. "These things were my Verna's. Can I show you her picture?" He reached into his wallet. The plastic photo insert was worn and torn. There was Verna on their wedding day.

George told me the story of the day they met and the life they built together. He spoke of their kids and travels. He shared with me her gradual health decline and how she wrote letters for every family member before her death.

"Oh, she spoiled me. She spoiled the hell out of me. She was my girl."

Full circle

The neighbor in the red coat came back into the room. She introduced herself to George; they hadn't seen one another in decades, but no one bothered with small talk or pleasantries. Instead, George told more stories. And as he cried, we cried. We stood still for a few moments in that upstairs room; it felt like the quiet of an empty sanctuary.

Eventually, George headed out to run errands. The neighbor left with the red coat. I lingered back with the belts.

After much indecision, I selected my favorites along with a long leather skirt then met Justin downstairs. We purchased our items and left.

As we drove away, I reflected. An estate sale is more than a venue for antiques and kitchenware. It is a glimpse into the stories of a home and the seasons of a life.

I don't know where Verna's belts have traveled in the past, but if George's remembrances are any hint, they've gone on a beautiful journey. It is an honor to think that now, with me in Minnesota, their story will continue.

Every Story
of Your Whole Life

I had one significant cleaning project to complete during my week of vacation. In addition to long morning hikes, lots of nature photography, and plenty of lunches with friends, I also wanted to tackle a task that had been waiting patiently in my garage.

Little did I know how good my organizing project would be for my soul.

There were three medium-sized storage totes. In them were the collected remnants of high school, college and seminary: stored notebooks, class syllabi, love letters, journals, and a host of other odds and ends.

I hadn't even seen most of it for more than a decade, so I figured it was time to downsize. My goal was to recycle at least 95 percent of the contents and keep the rest in the form of a scrapbook.

As I opened the first tote, it only took a few minutes for the tears to start welling up. I dug through the contents and came across a stack of greeting cards from my high school graduation. One in particular was signed by Grandma Verona, in her lovely penmanship. The G on Grandma was the perfect combination of curls and swoops.

In addition to a thoughtful card, she included a special note on scratch paper. "Could you please send me a copy of your graduation speech? I couldn't hear it very well in the gym, and I would love to read it. But only if you have time."

I can't remember for certain if I gave her a copy of my speech, but I sure hope and pray that I did. The ten-year anniversary of her death is today. The cycles of grief are certainly unpredictable; lately I miss her more than ever.

Throughout her life, she was an active member of her Lutheran congregation in Waterloo, Iowa. She quilted, made pies, and served on the funeral committee of her church. Looking back, I wish I had asked her about the many ways she lived her life of faith.

I always loved spending time with Grandma, but I don't remember asking many questions. I mostly remember piano playing, Uno games, and an endless supply of Fruit Roll-Ups. I was 19 when she died and still not fully adept at soaking in the wisdom of my elders.

If I could write her a note on scratch paper today, I'd say: "Grandma, could we please meet for coffee at your house? I want to hear every story of your whole life. Let's start at the beginning."

By the end of my third day of vacation, I completed my organizing project. It was more enjoyable than I expected. I was able to recycle about 90 percent of the contents.

Of course, I didn't recycle everything. I'm holding onto the stack of letters and cards I've received from friends and family over the years. And I've decided that I'm no longer going to keep them in the garage.

Instead, I found a nice basket, and I'm keeping them in my bedroom. They remind me of all the encouragement, love and prayers that have led me to today.

My cleaning project turned out to be more than an exercise in clearing out extra garage space. It also became a time to give thanks for the people in my life — past and present — who have shown me the love of God in a great multitude of ways.

Pride, the Swan

Her name is Pride. She is a swan and lives on the grounds of a botanical garden. My friend, Joy, and I saw her on a recent excursion. We were following the path and taking note of the different flowers and trees.

We came upon a fountain, and near it sat a beautiful white swan, all curled up with her beak buried in her feathers. I've seen the geese at Silver Lake in a similar position when they get chilly, but this seemed different. It was as if the swan was avoiding contact with the rest of the world.

As we stepped closer, it was clear that the bird was not particularly interested in our company. She refused to budge from her preferred position. As we stood a couple feet from her, an employee from the garden wandered away from her tour group and walked toward us. "That's Pride. She just returned after being gone for ten years. But now she keeps escaping."

Wondering what she meant by that comment, I asked, "Escaping to other parts of the property?"

"No, she leaves completely. She crosses that busy highway, and then we have to go and get her wherever she ends up. Pride had a best friend swan who recently died of old age. She's been sad ever since. We're hoping to get a new female friend for her very soon."

Then the woman journeyed on while my friend and I stood looking at Pride, expressing a few encouraging words. "It will get better, Pride. They're going to find you a friend."

It wasn't hard to understand how tempting it must have been for the swan to saunter up the nearby hill, cross the busy highway, and continue her search for happiness. She was lonely.

Friendships aren't a big deal just for swans. They're important for people, too. Companionship is central to a healthy life. At different stages and ages, however, it's easy to downplay the importance of friendships.

In the busy years of child-raising and full schedules, it's common to hear, "Friendships are so hard to maintain. Life is too busy right now." Or, in the more advanced years of life, it's normal to be saddened by the realities of how friendships change when ailments and memory loss come into play.

Yet, as many changes that life can bring to friendships, that doesn't alter their importance. Life-giving friendships have deep meaning!

The changes we face are not so different from those faced by Pride the Swan. We face all kinds of transitions that can reshape our friendships. Sometimes it's a move to a new town, a diagnosis, a death, or a career change.

Regardless of what the hurdles might be, there are always opportunities to nourish meaningful friendships. It takes effort and intention, but it's worth it.

God created human beings in such a way that community and connectedness have great value.

So even in the toughest of times, when we feel like burying our beaks into our feathers, may hope fill our hearts. Companionship is possible in a multitude of ways, and, in every stage of life, there are friendships to be formed.

Acknowledgements

The opportunity to write and publish a book is a wondrous, precious gift, and I am profoundly grateful. I would like to specifically thank:

Holy Spirit: Thank you for being the source of all creativity, ideas and possibilities. Thank you for weaving strands of hope throughout every season of my life and teaching me to use words to explore ideas. I am infinitely thankful for a chance to exist on this mysterious planet.

Mom: You are my greatest inspiration. Thank you for always modeling compassion and curiosity. Thank you for encouraging me to dream, explore and create each day.

Justin: You continually teach me about love and true partnership. Thank you for all the ways you plant seeds of thoughtfulness, creativity and loyalty in the universe. As we said in our wedding vows two years ago, I claim again today: To love you and be loved by you is my greatest joy and privilege.

Josh and Sweta: Brother and Behen, thank you for being such an important and grounding part of my life. Josh, you're a thoughtful, hilarious, supportive brother, and I feel grateful for the gift of being your big sister. Sweta, your presence in our family has been a transformative force of love and connectedness.

Finn the Redbone Coonhound: I wish you could read, buddy. I don't deserve you, dear dog, but I sure do love you. It's hard to describe how much your presence in my days has rewired my heart. Thanks for forgiving me for thinking I'd never become a dog person. You and Justin are my perfect surprises, and I'm so glad you both came into my life.

Stolls: My precious bonus family! Marriage is a gift on so many levels, and getting to journey through life with you is a gift that keeps on giving. Thank you for welcoming me into your family and for welcoming my family into your family, too. Your hospitality and care give me courage to be myself.

Hundleys: To my aunts, uncles and cousins: I'm grateful we're part of the same family tree. Thank you for your support and encouragement. I'm glad we share the same ancestors, and I'm also excessively thankful we get to be on this planet at the same time.

Carsons: Thank you to my dad and the entire Carson crew. Your love and thoughtfulness mean so much to me, and I'm thankful for your presence in my life.

Brian Scott and 9 Foot Voice: Your encouragement about my writing has been a profoundly impactful force in my life. Thanks for believing in me, for being a gifted editor, and for publishing my first book! I'm thankful for your friendship, thoughtfulness and support.

Jeff Pieters and the staff of the Rochester Post-Bulletin: Jeff, thank you for being my editor at the Post-Bulletin all these years! You are supportive and encouraging. You empower me to try new things, and you believe in my voice. Thank you! And thanks to the Post-Bulletin for giving me space in the paper to explore ideas about life and faith every week.

Doug McGill and the Rochester Meditation Center: Several years ago, I took a 6-week course called "Introduction to Mindfulness" and it altered the course of my life. Doug, thanks for empowering me to live in an entirely new kind of relationship with my thoughts and feelings.

Friends and roommates in college and seminary: I've been fortunate to have an outstanding cadre of compassionate, motivated, justice-oriented friends my whole life! Thank you, friends and roomies, for all you've shown me about living with a heart wide open.

The faculty and staff of Dunkerton High School, Wartburg College and the Lutheran School of Theology at Chicago: Learning is my favorite part of existence, and I owe much of that passion to all of you. I'm thankful for your commitment to teach in engaging, collaborative ways. Thank you for all the support you've shown every step of the way!

The staff of the Southeastern Minnesota Synod: It has been a joy to serve with you. We've journeyed through a lot together. What a gift it is when colleagues become family. Thank you for always encouraging me to show up in my work each day as my whole, authentic self.

The people of Zion Lutheran Church in Stewartville, MN and Our Redeemer Lutheran Church in Marion, IL: You are the two communities of faith that have taught me the most about what it means to be community. Thank you for trusting me with the role of serving as pastor and pastoral intern in your midst. Thank you for teaching me about Jesus, agape, resilience, hope and the church.

Librarians, Scientists, Historians, Poets and Pastors: Thank you for the ways you empower people to learn and grow in a complicated universe. Your work matters and it makes a significant impact.

About the Author

Emily Carson lives in Rochester, Minnesota with her husband, Justin, and their redbone coonhound, Finn. She is an ordained Lutheran pastor. Emily enjoys writing, speaking and exploring the world with a notebook in one hand and a camera in the other.

Visit her website for links to her blog, newsletter and social media accounts: www.emilyannecarson.com.

Made in the USA
Lexington, KY
01 December 2019